The Sword
in the Stone

Written by Mary Hoffman
Illustrated by Dante Ginerva

It was midnight. Merlin the wizard waited at the gate of King Uther Pendragon's castle.

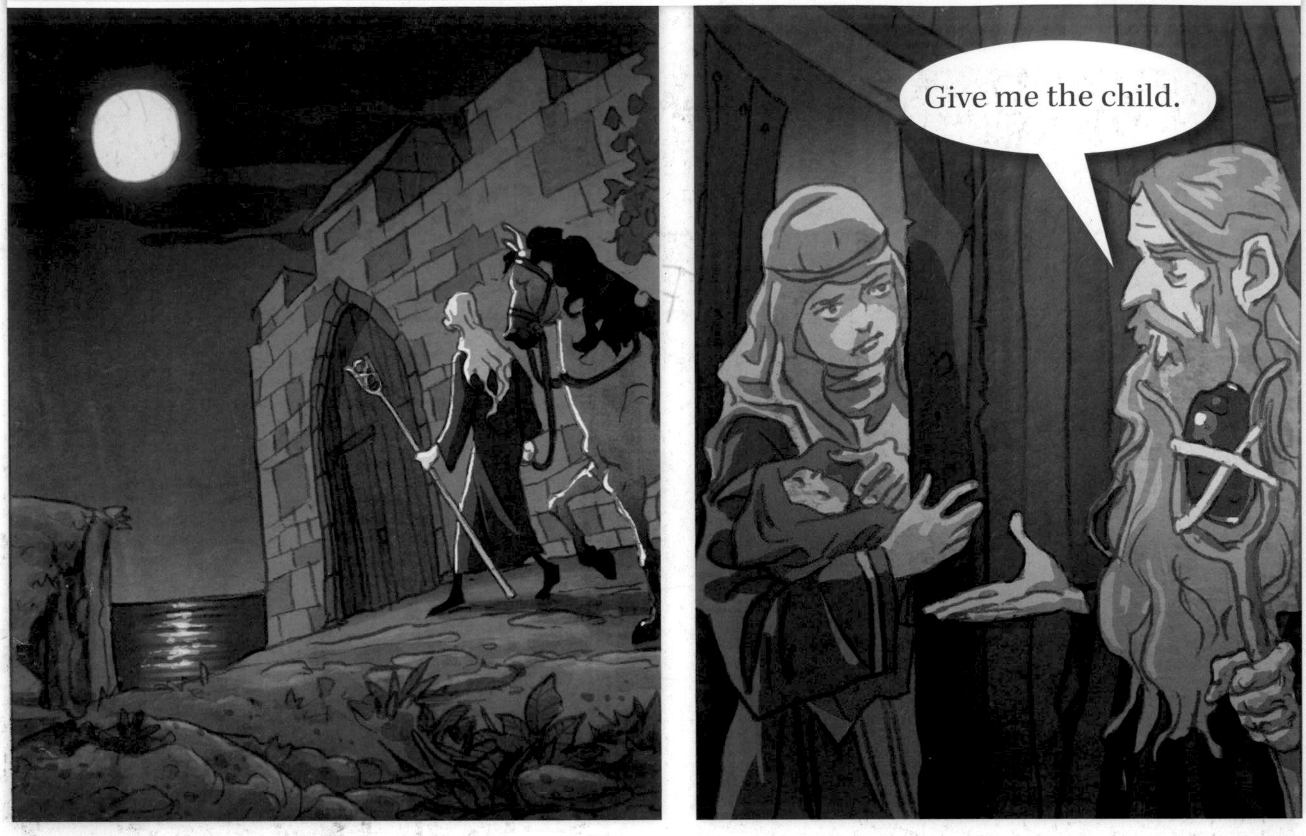
Give me the child.

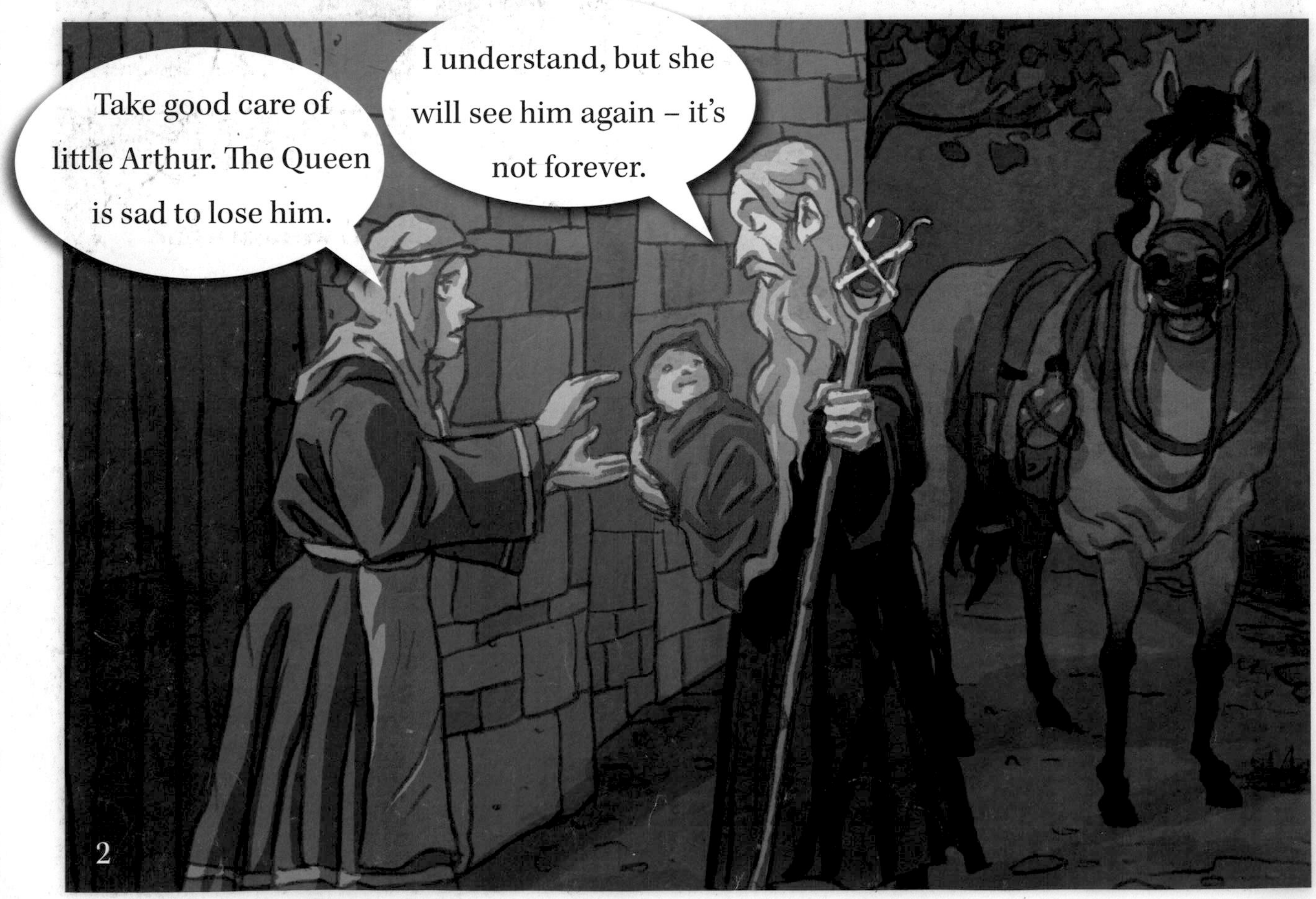
Take good care of little Arthur. The Queen is sad to lose him.
I understand, but she will see him again – it's not forever.

Merlin mounted his horse and rode with the baby boy in his arms. After many hours, he reached the castle of Sir Ector and his wife, Lady Anna.

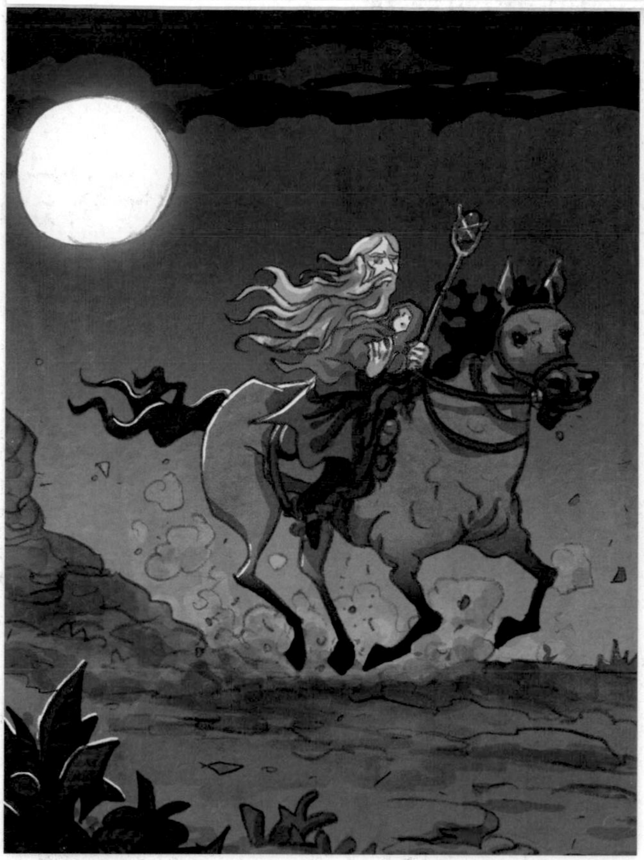

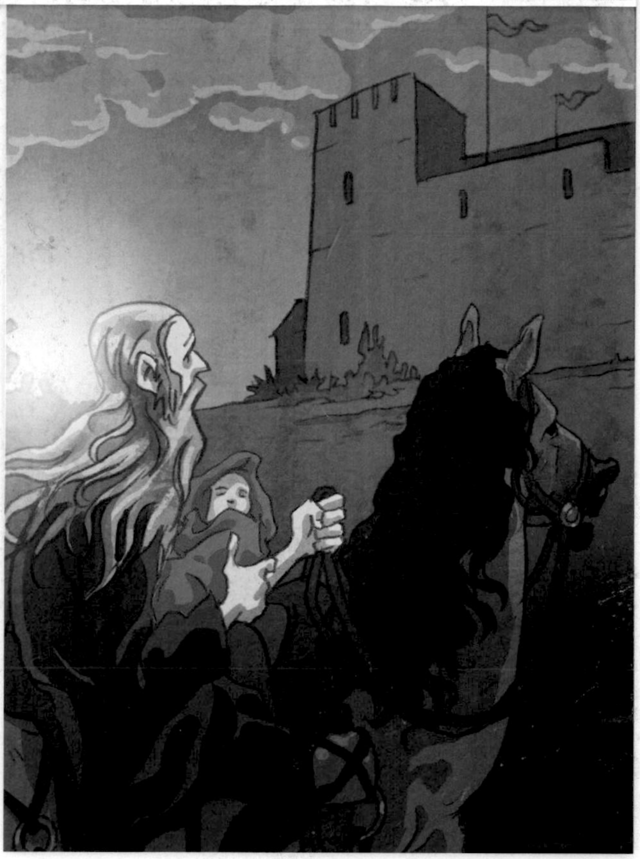

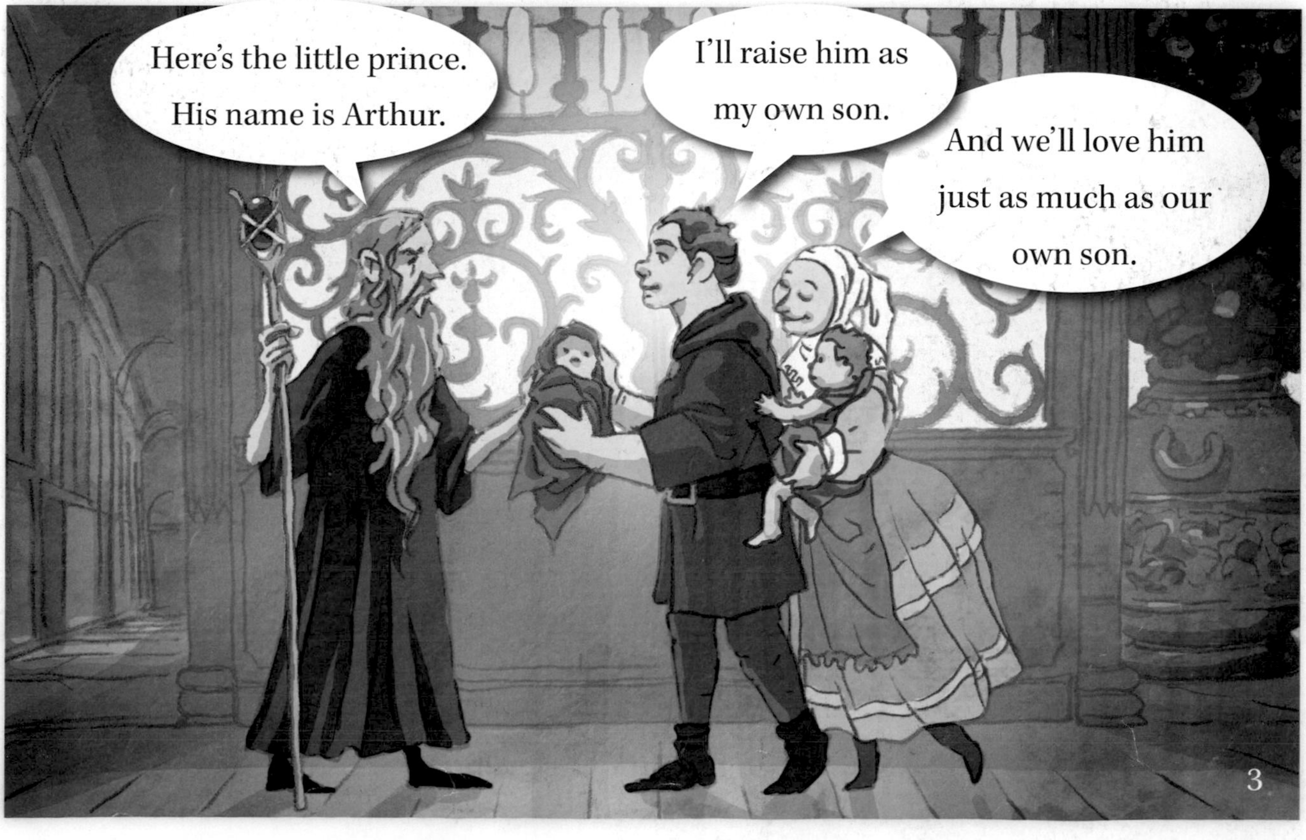
Here's the little prince. His name is Arthur.
I'll raise him as my own son.
And we'll love him just as much as our own son.

Two years later, King Uther Pendragon became very sick – now more than ever he needed the support and advice of the wise wizard Merlin. At the same time, his lands were invaded by lords from the north.

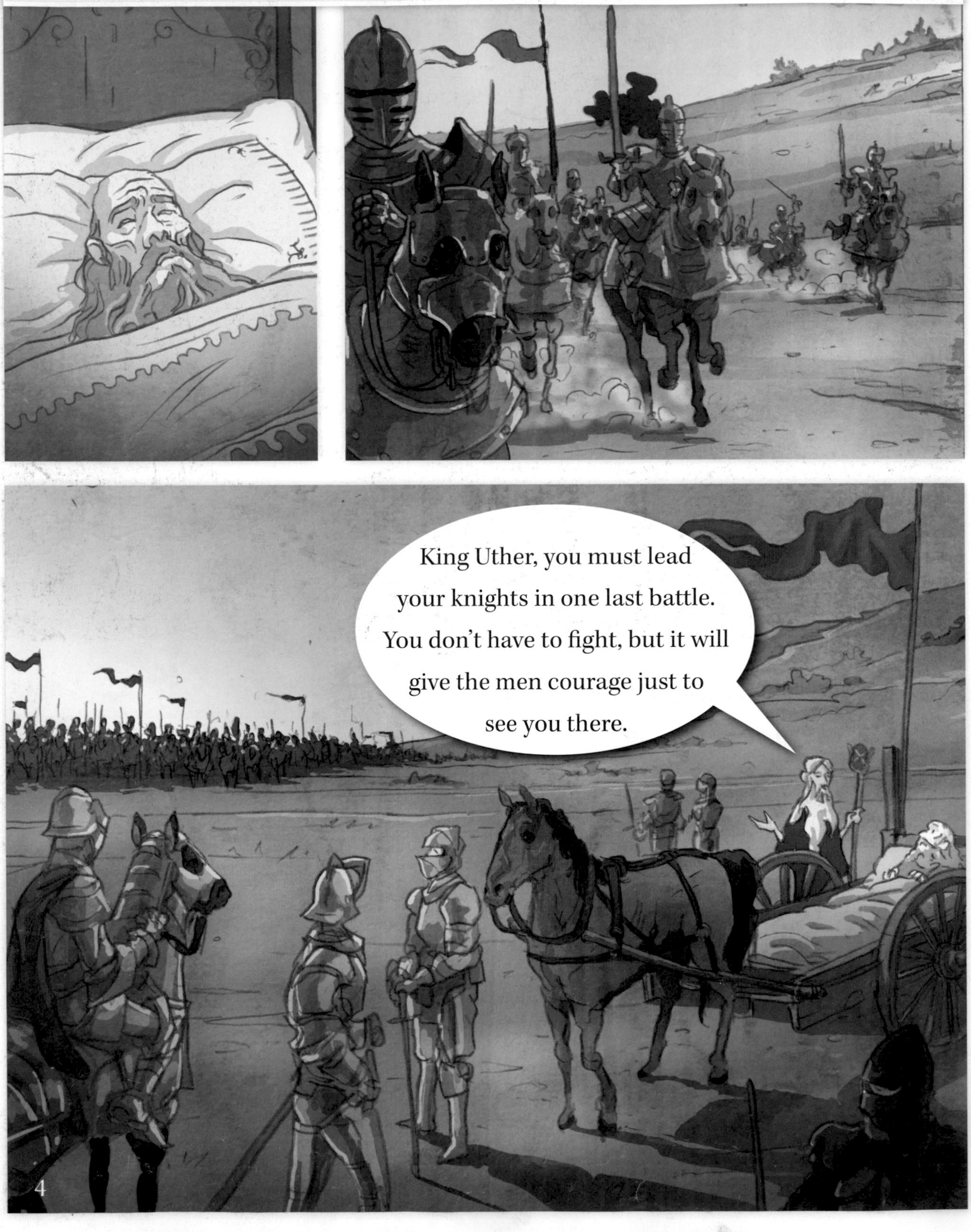
King Uther, you must lead your knights in one last battle. You don't have to fight, but it will give the men courage just to see you there.

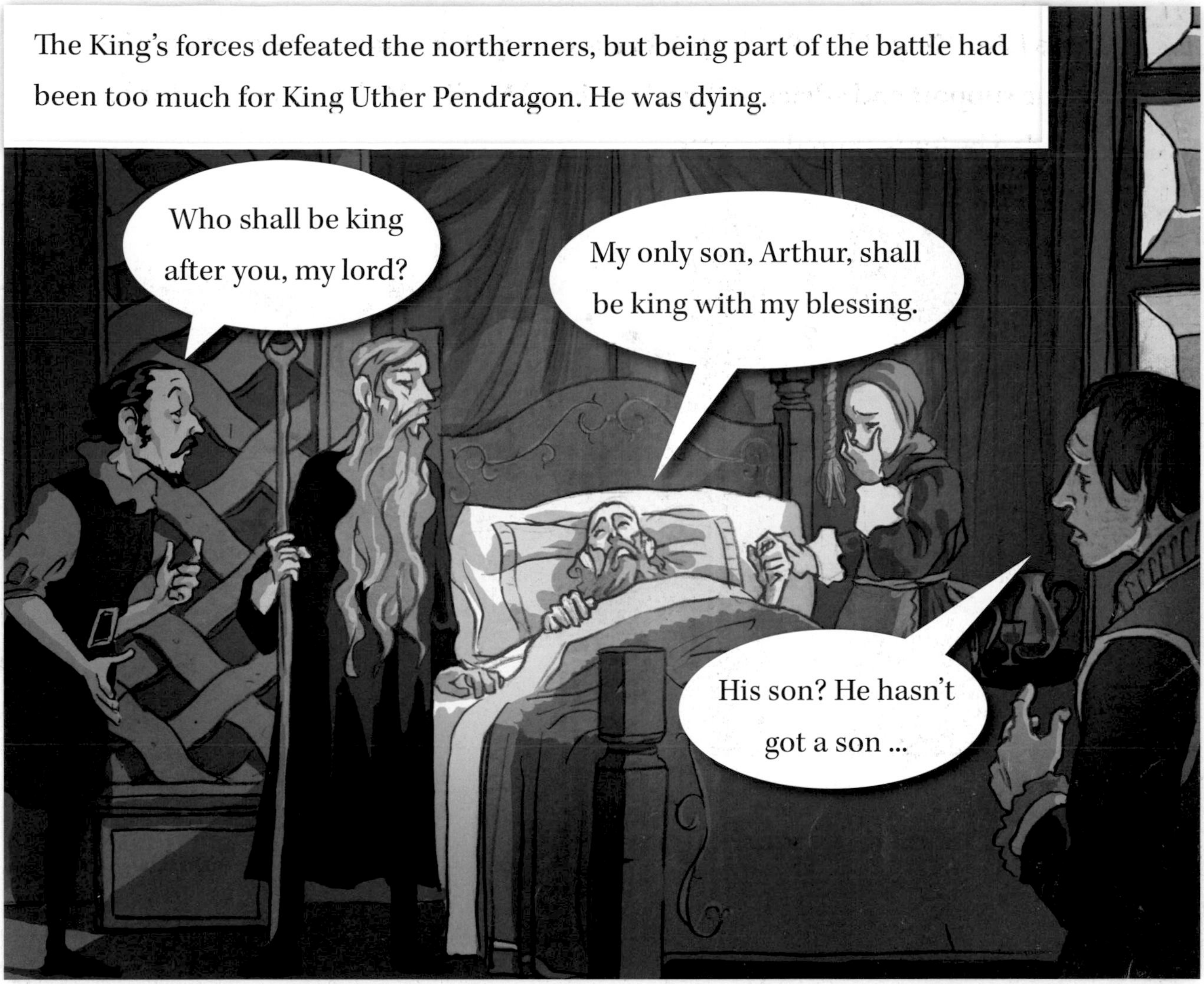
The King's forces defeated the northerners, but being part of the battle had been too much for King Uther Pendragon. He was dying.
Who shall be king after you, my lord?
My only son, Arthur, shall be king with my blessing.
His son? He hasn't got a son ...

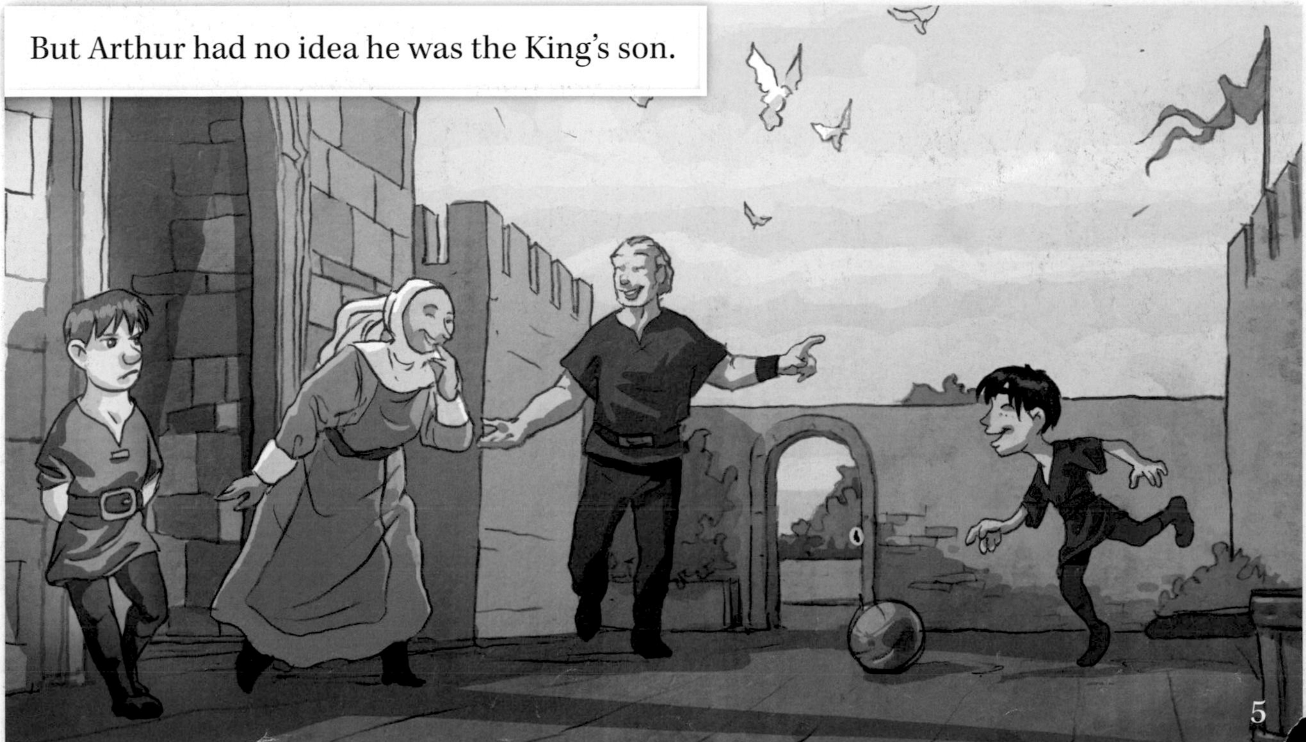
But Arthur had no idea he was the King's son.

After the old King died, England was at war for many years because no one knew who should be king and there was no one in charge of the country.

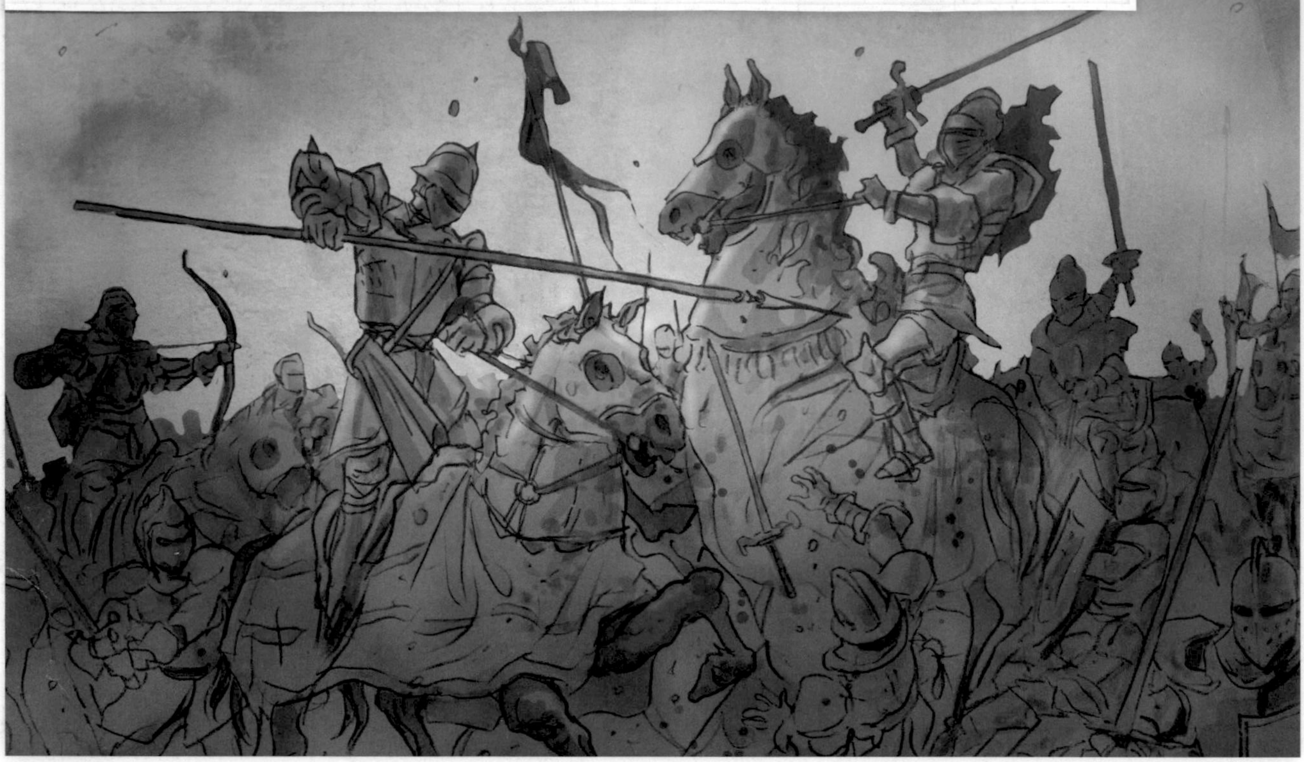

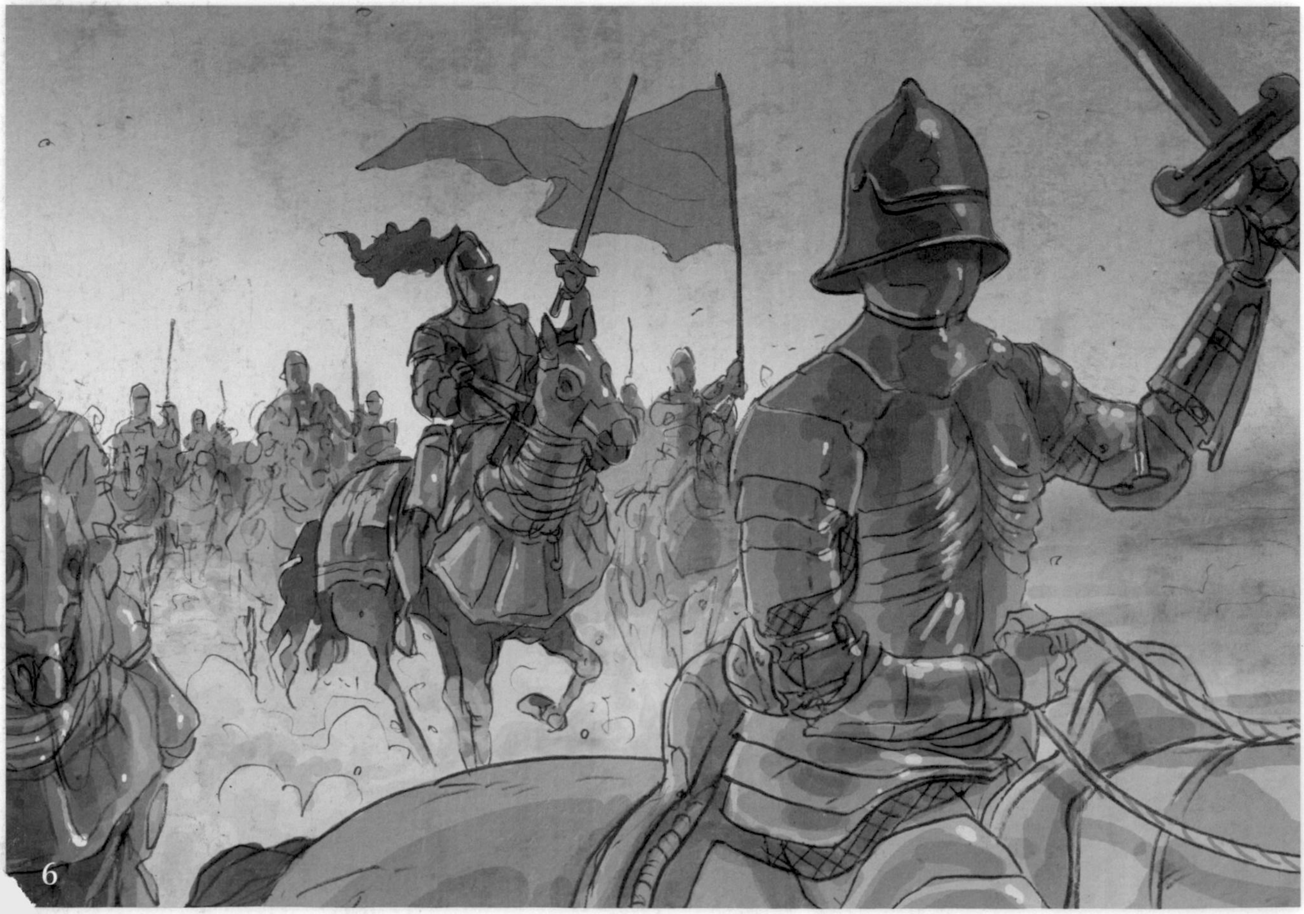

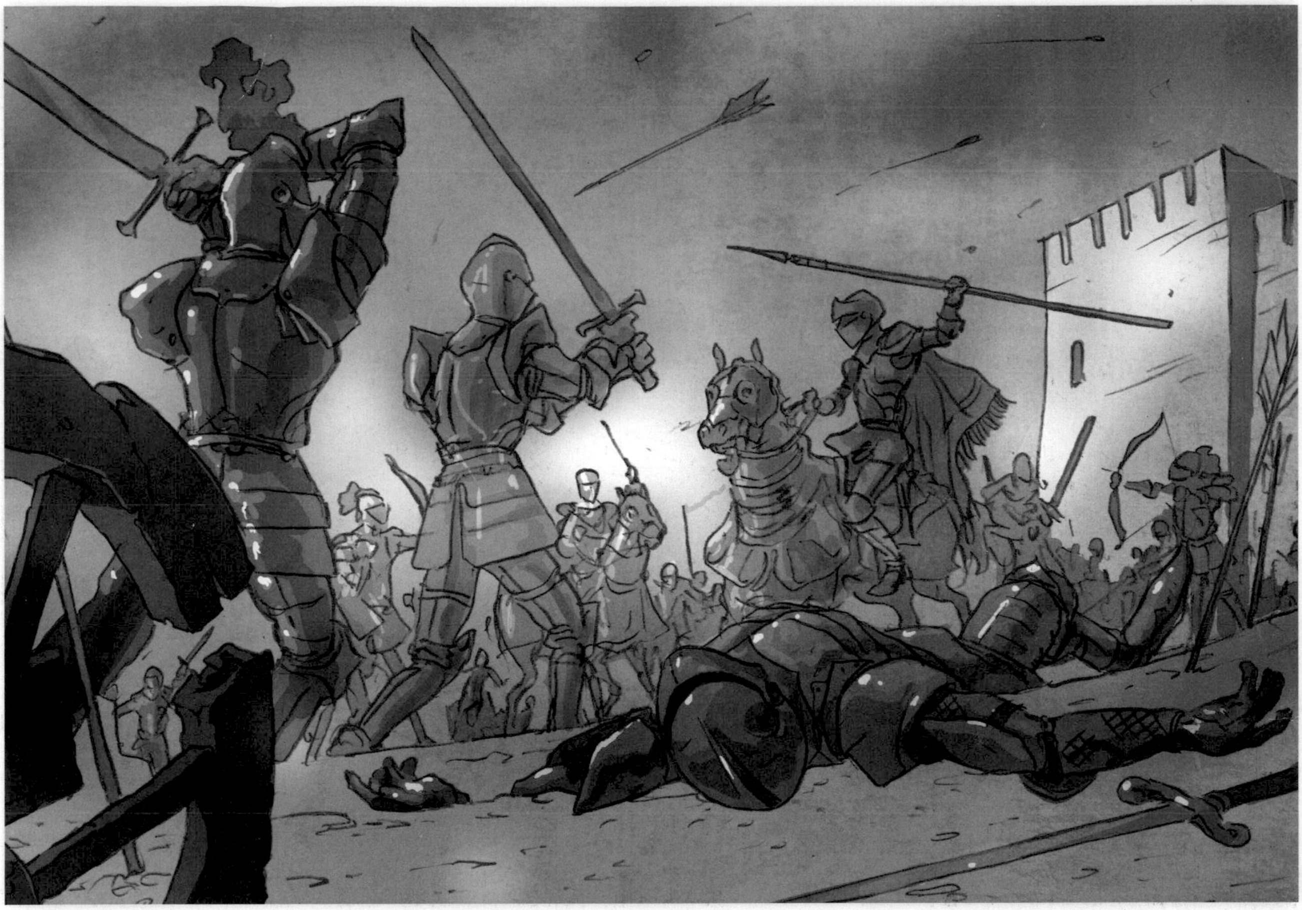

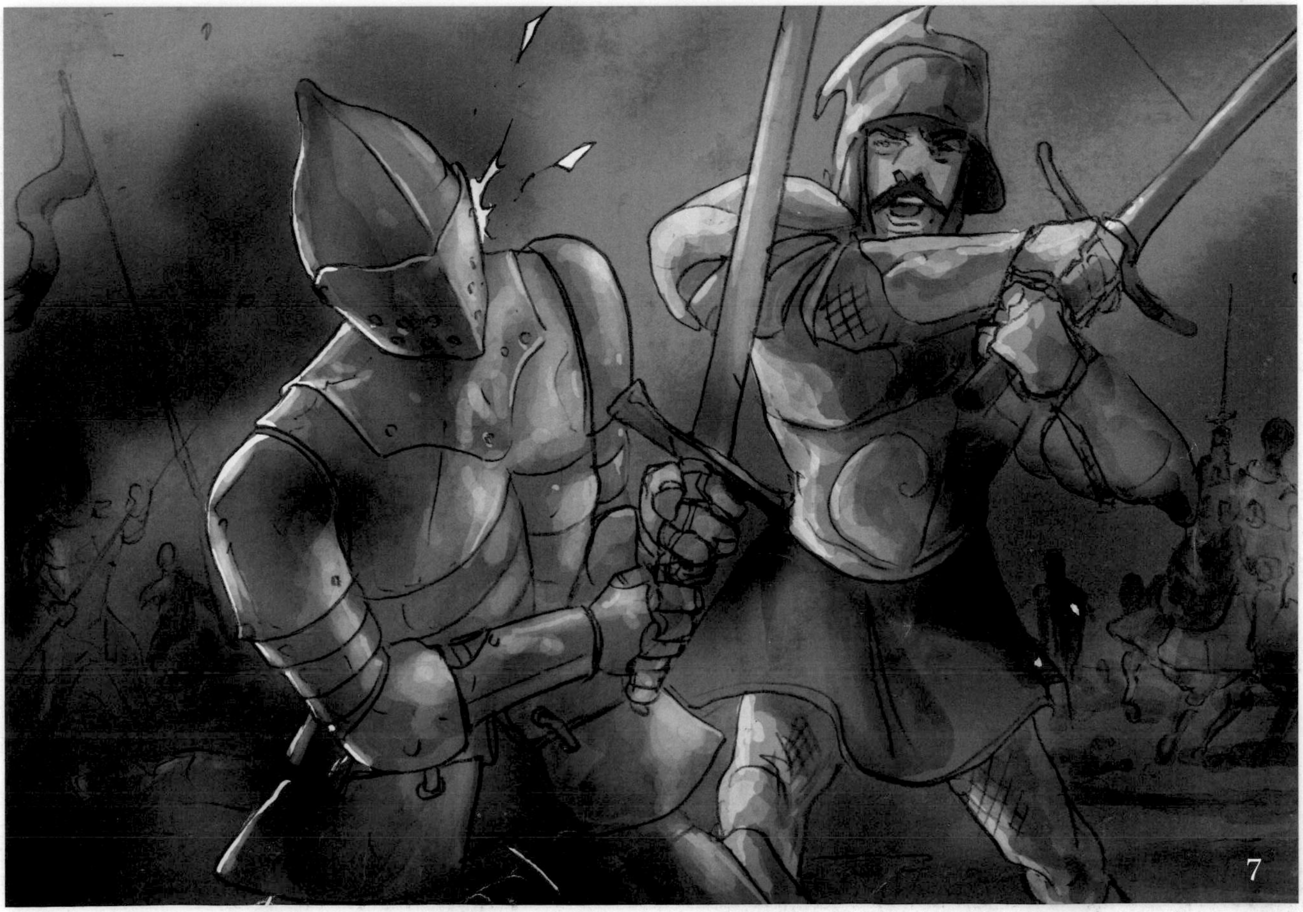

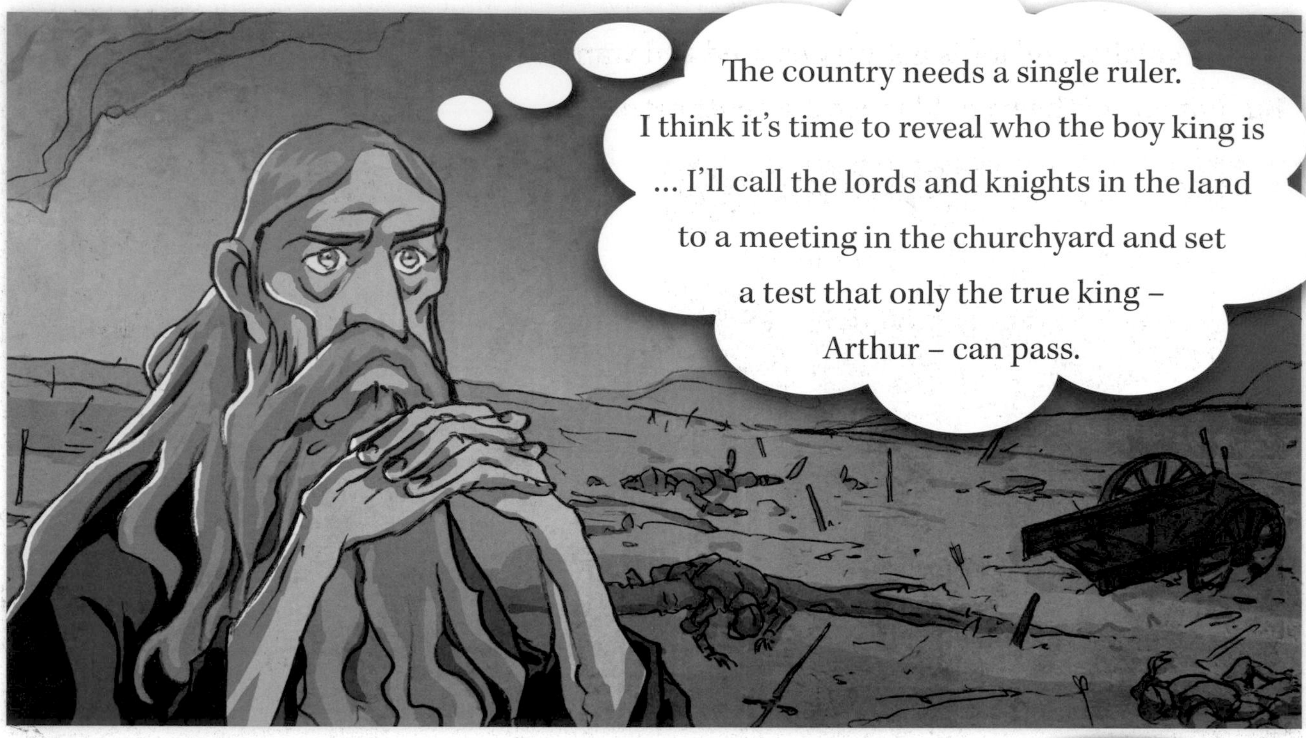
The country needs a single ruler. I think it's time to reveal who the boy king is ... I'll call the lords and knights in the land to a meeting in the churchyard and set a test that only the true king – Arthur – can pass.

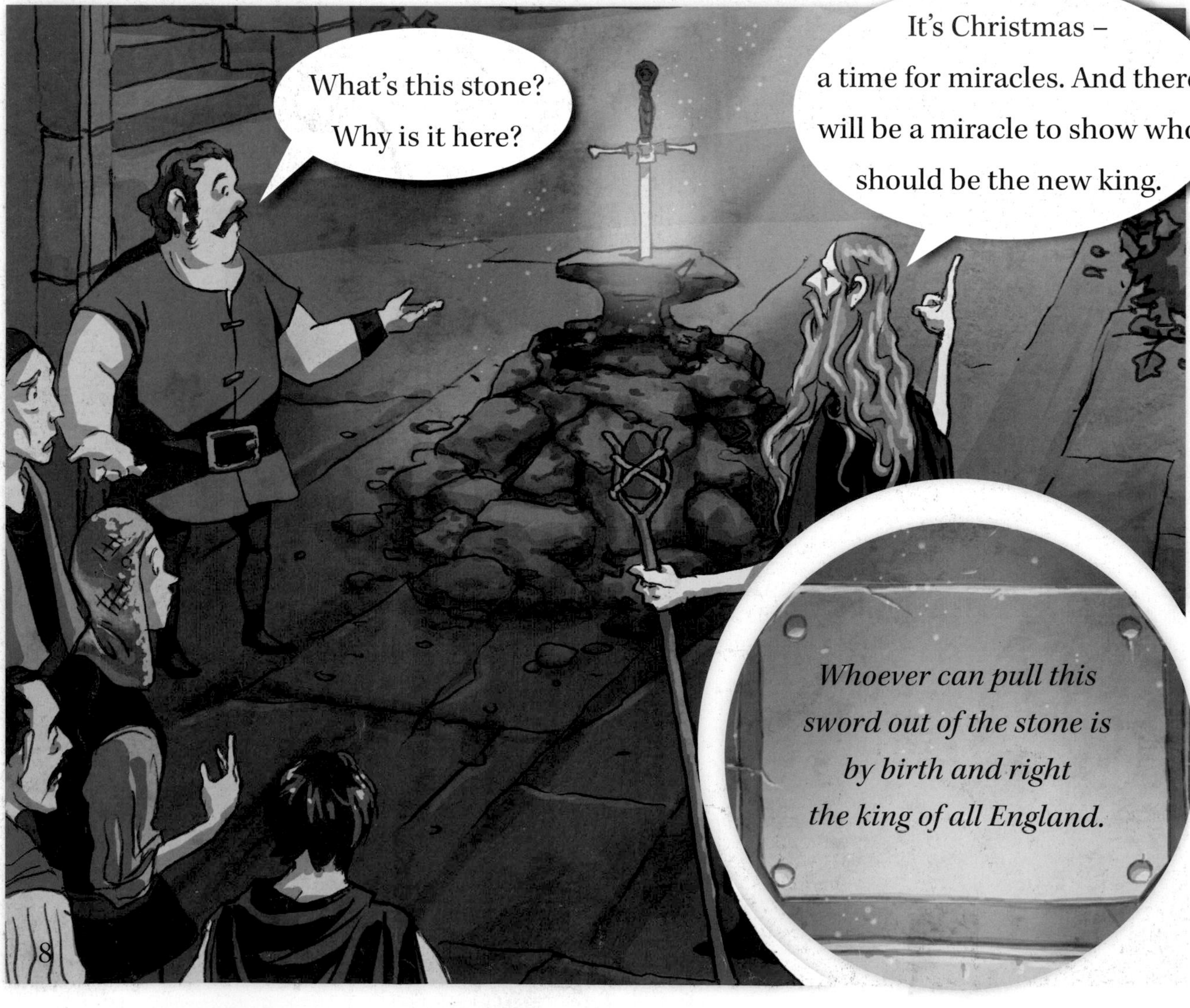
What's this stone? Why is it here?
It's Christmas – a time for miracles. And there will be a miracle to show who should be the new king.
Whoever can pull this sword out of the stone is by birth and right the king of all England.

All the knights and lords got very excited and wanted to pull out the sword. But not one of them could move it a centimetre.

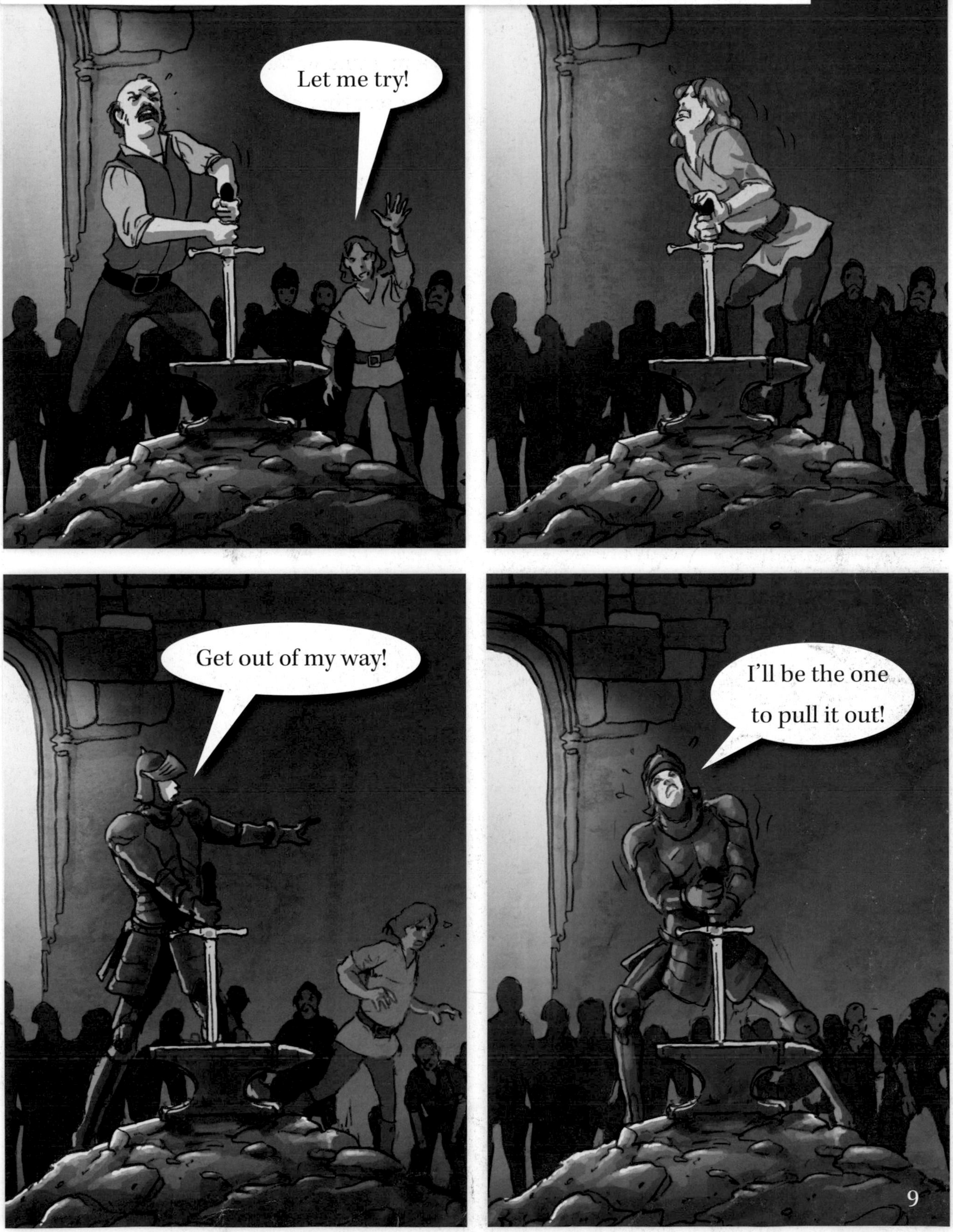
Let me try!
Get out of my way!
I'll be the one to pull it out!

No one could pull out the sword so Merlin decided that a great tournament, with archery and swordfights, would be held on New Year's Day. He hoped it would encourage more knights and lords to come to London to test themselves with the sword.

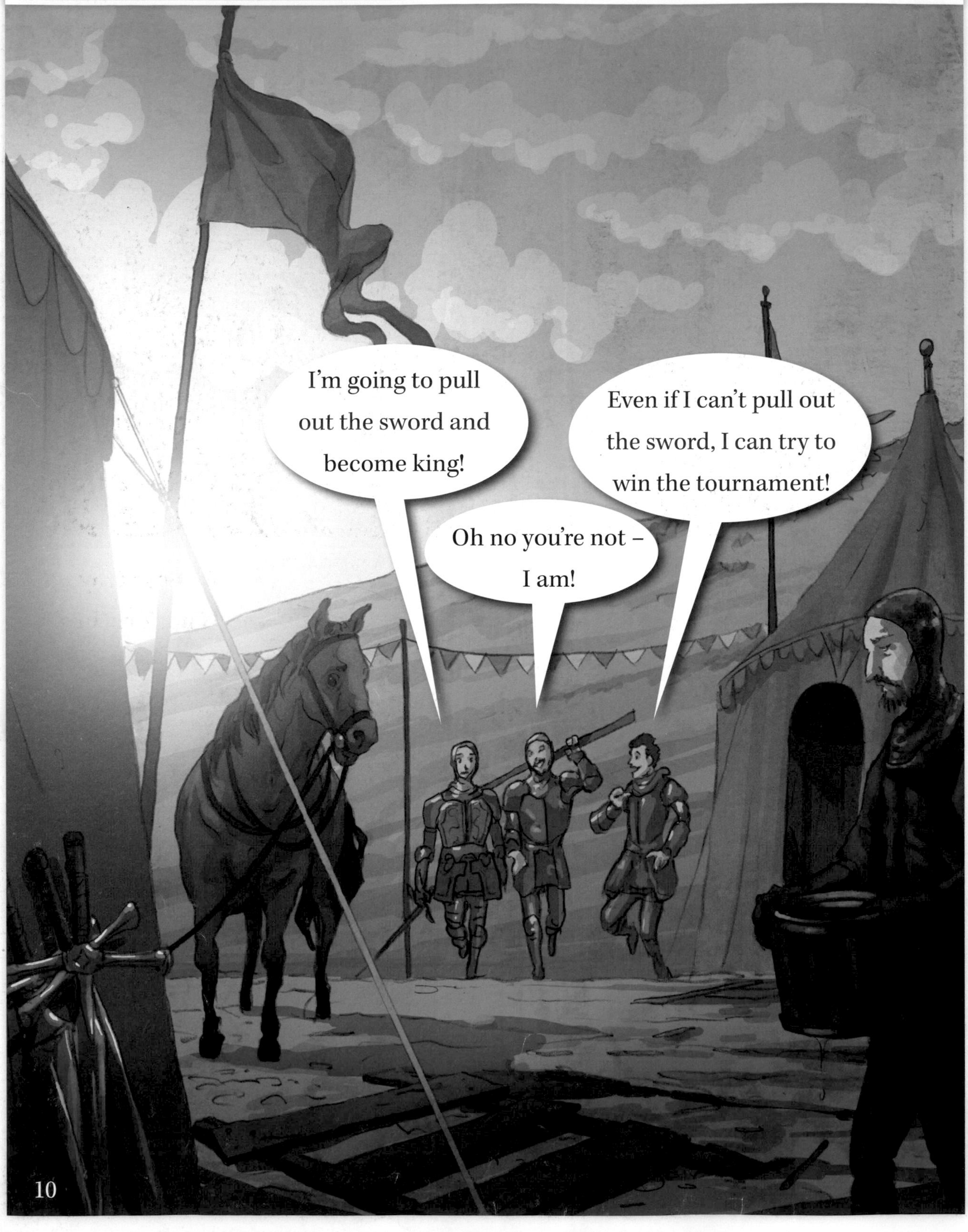
I'm going to pull out the sword and become king!
Oh no you're not – I am!
Even if I can't pull out the sword, I can try to win the tournament!

Sir Ector brought his two sons, Kay and Arthur, to the tournament. Arthur had no idea Ector wasn't his real father – the two boys believed they were brothers.

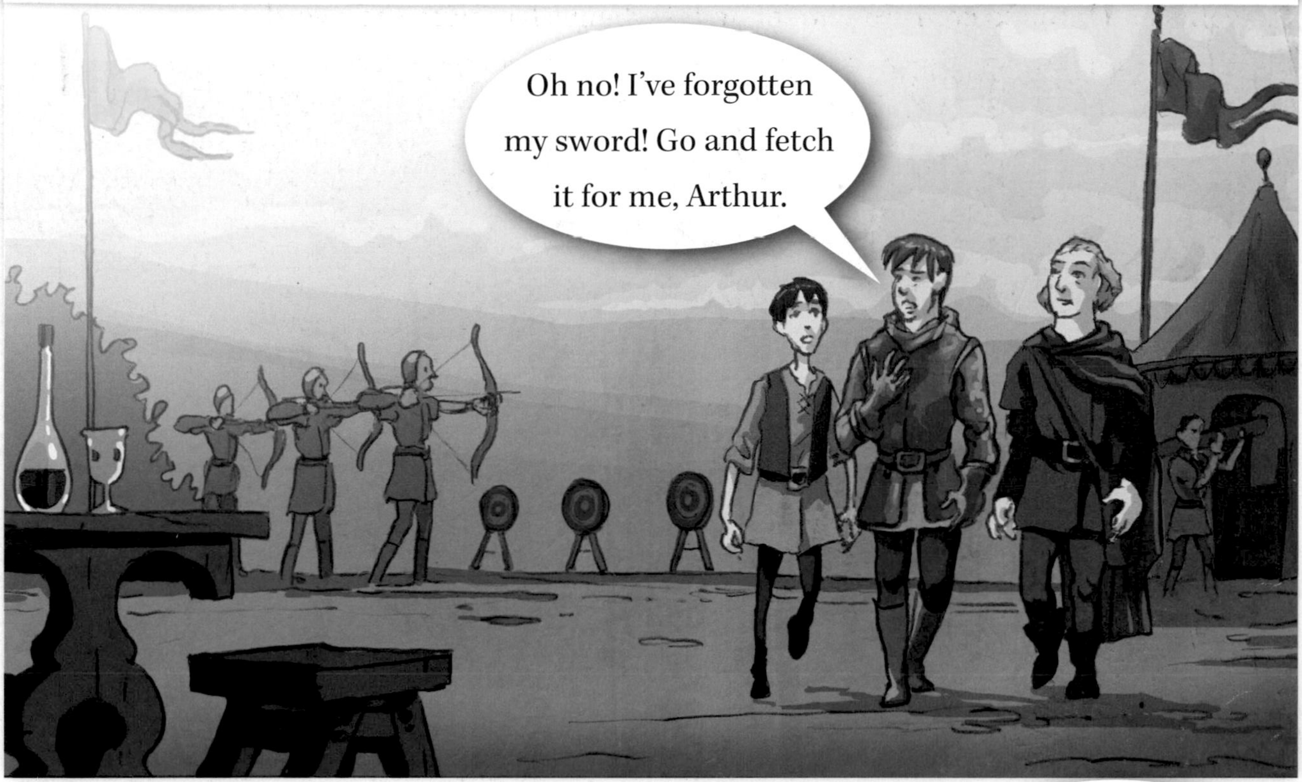
Oh no! I've forgotten my sword! Go and fetch it for me, Arthur.

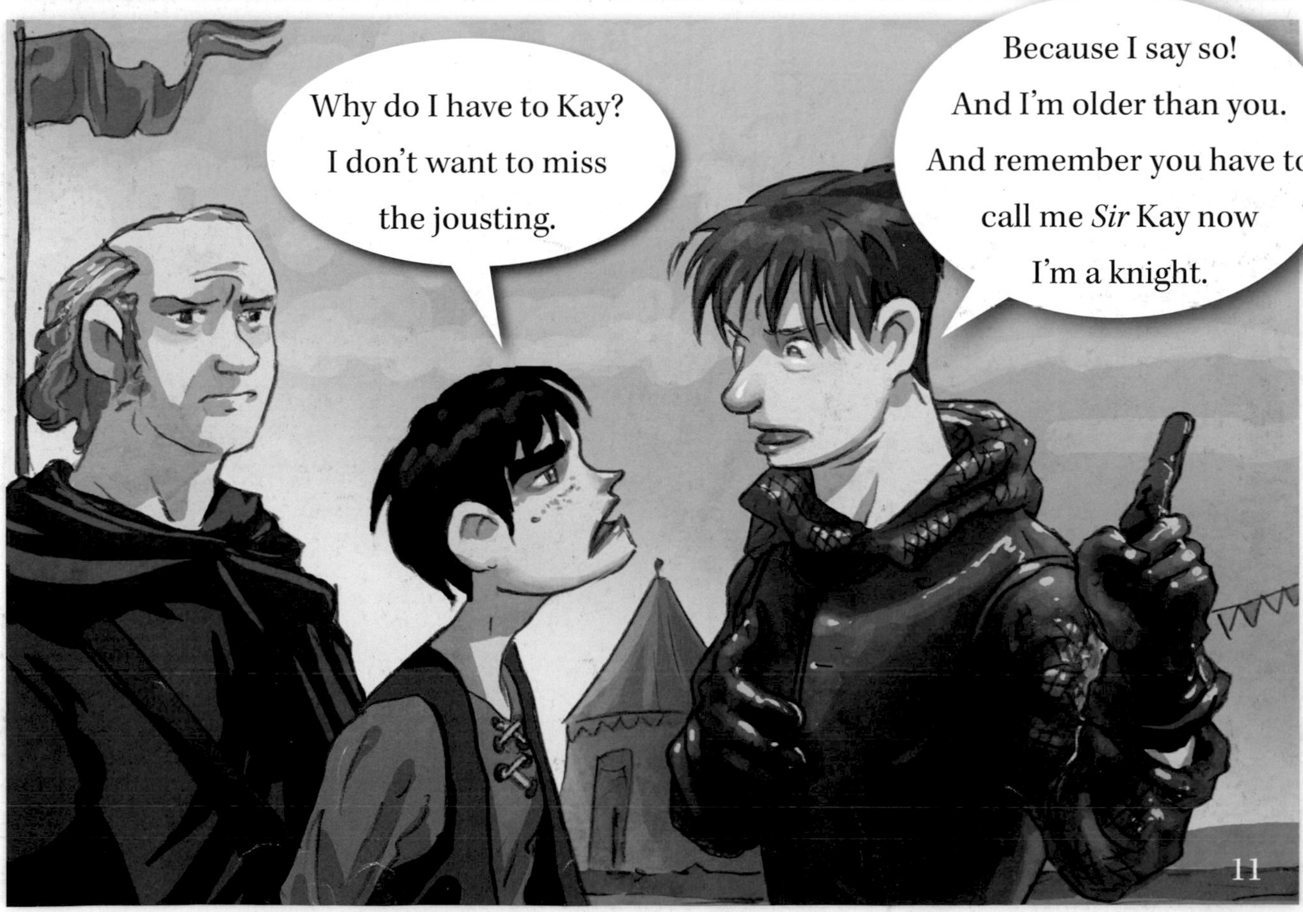
Why do I have to Kay? I don't want to miss the jousting.
Because I say so! And I'm older than you. And remember you have to call me *Sir* Kay now I'm a knight.

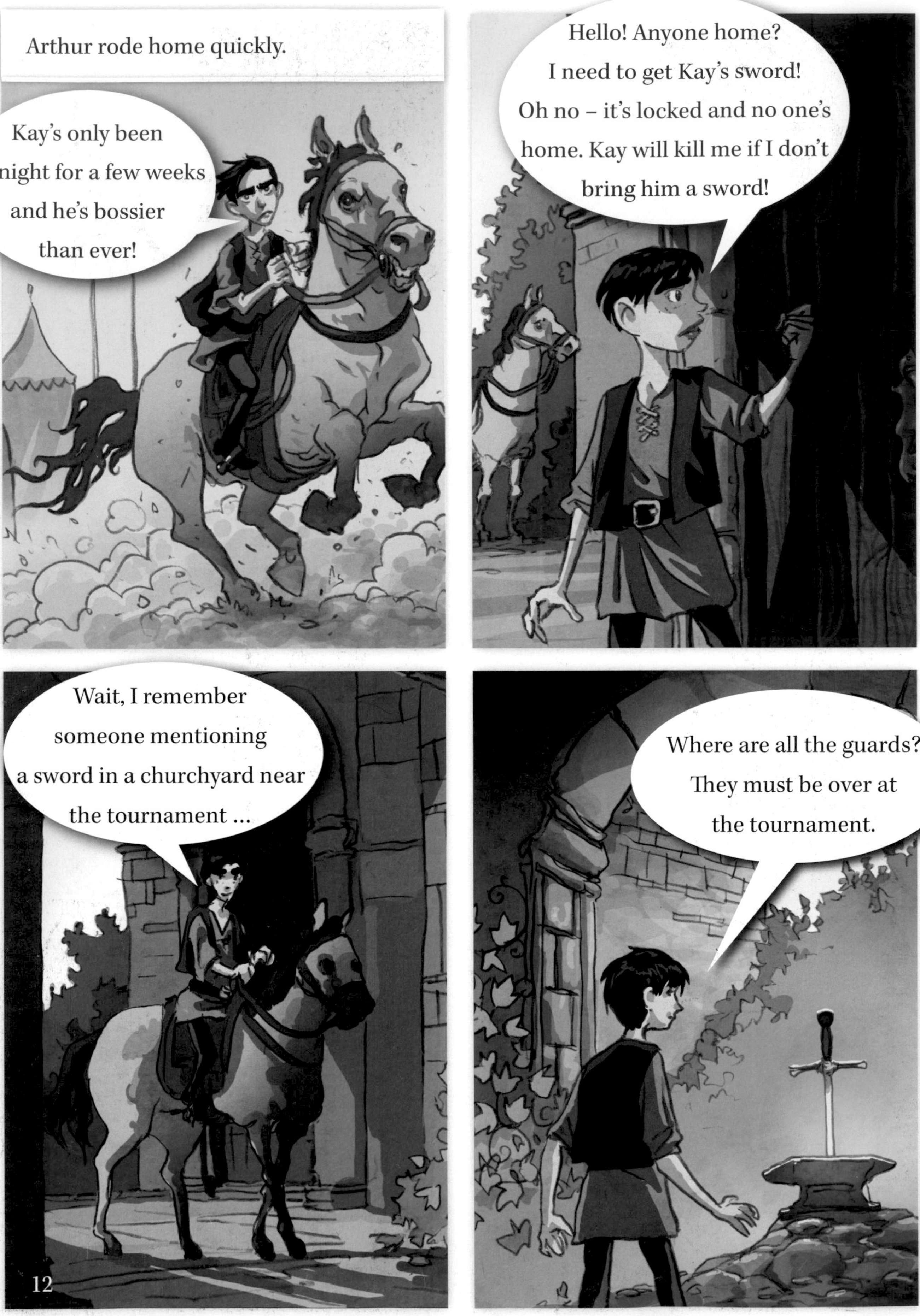
Arthur rode home quickly.
Kay's only been a knight for a few weeks and he's bossier than ever!
Hello! Anyone home? I need to get Kay's sword! Oh no – it's locked and no one's home. Kay will kill me if I don't bring him a sword!
Wait, I remember someone mentioning a sword in a churchyard near the tournament …
Where are all the guards? They must be over at the tournament.

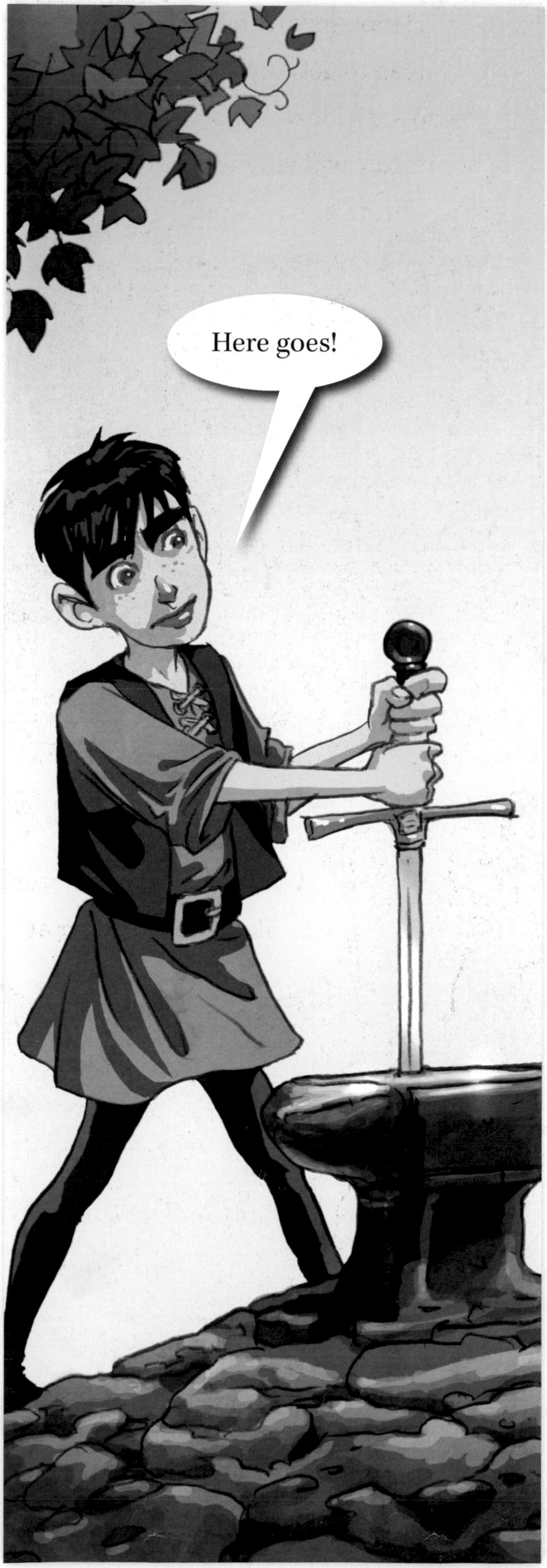
Here goes!

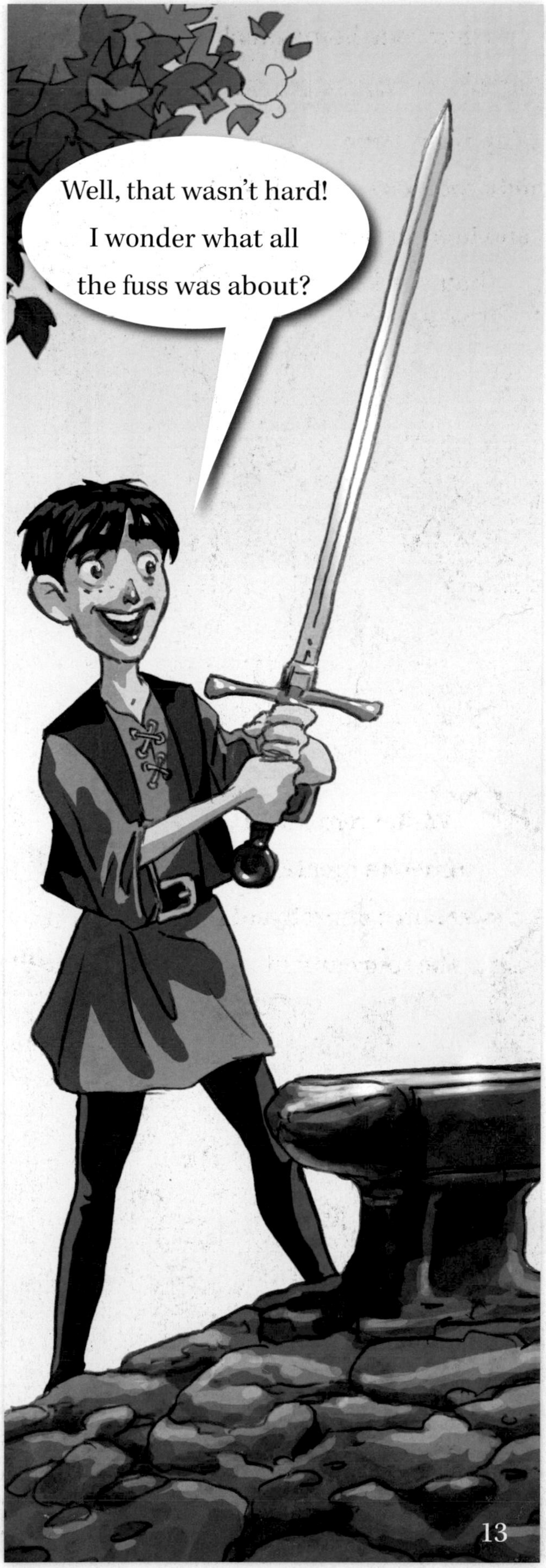
Well, that wasn't hard! I wonder what all the fuss was about?

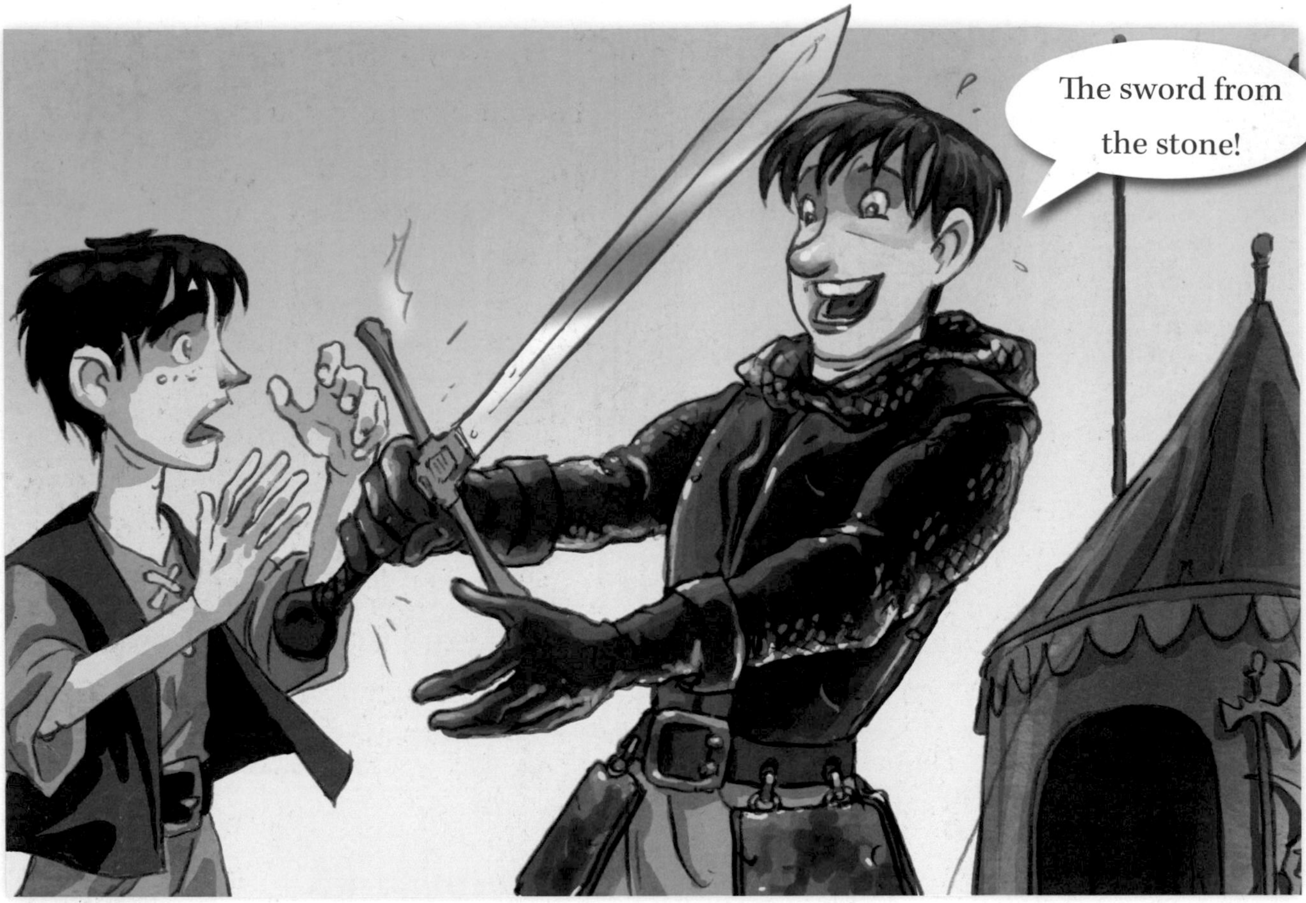
The sword from the stone!

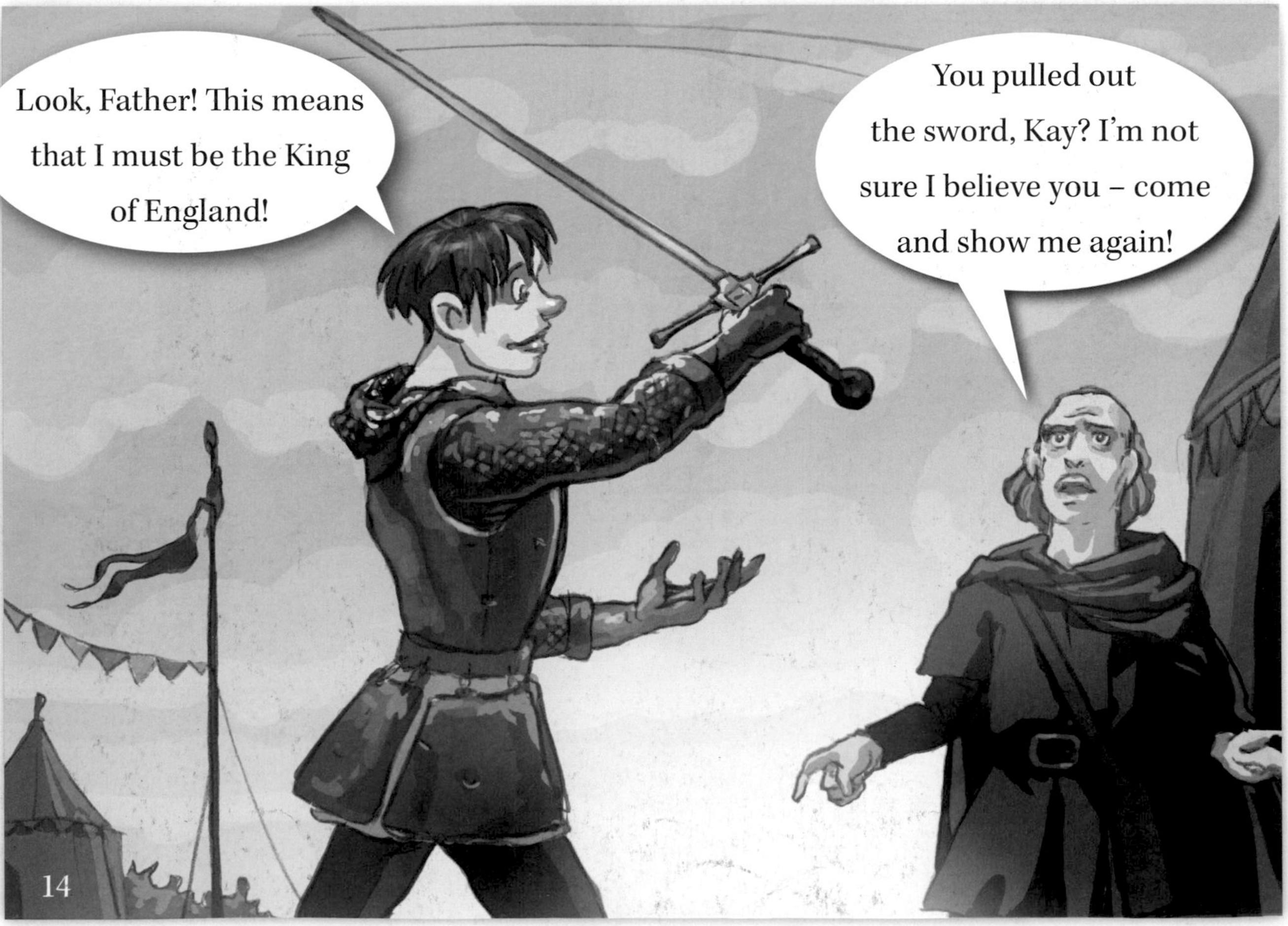
Look, Father! This means that I must be the King of England!
You pulled out the sword, Kay? I'm not sure I believe you – come and show me again!

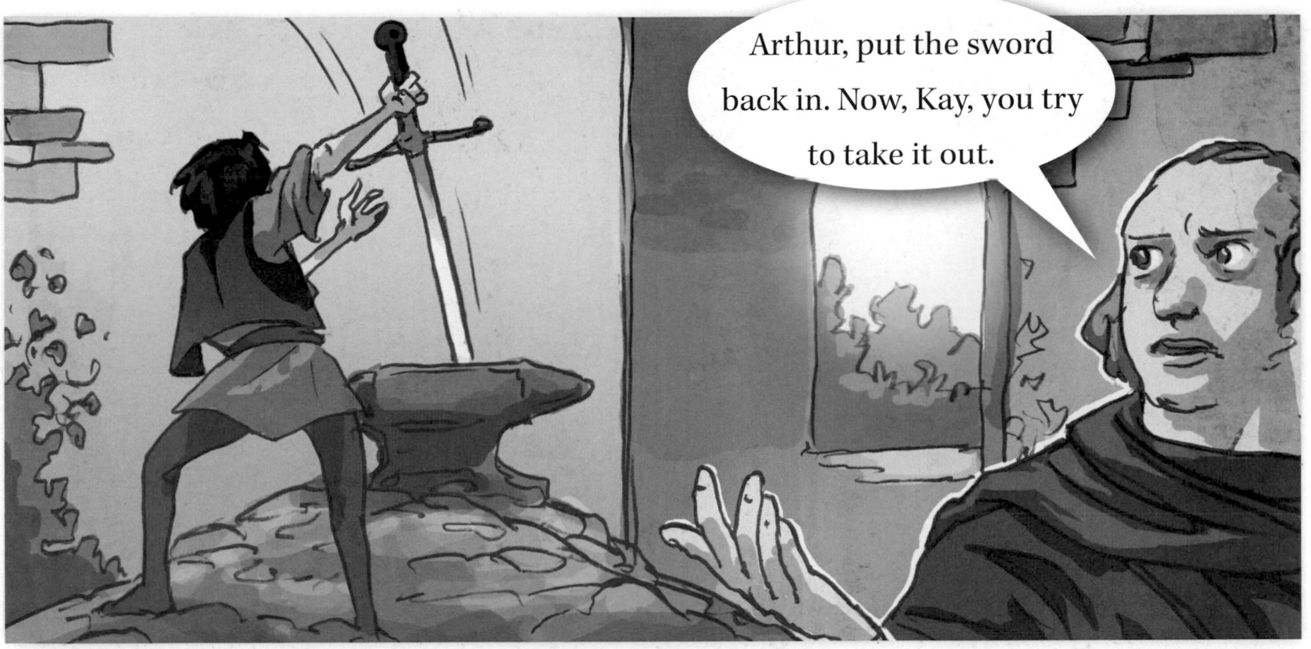
Arthur, put the sword back in. Now, Kay, you try to take it out.

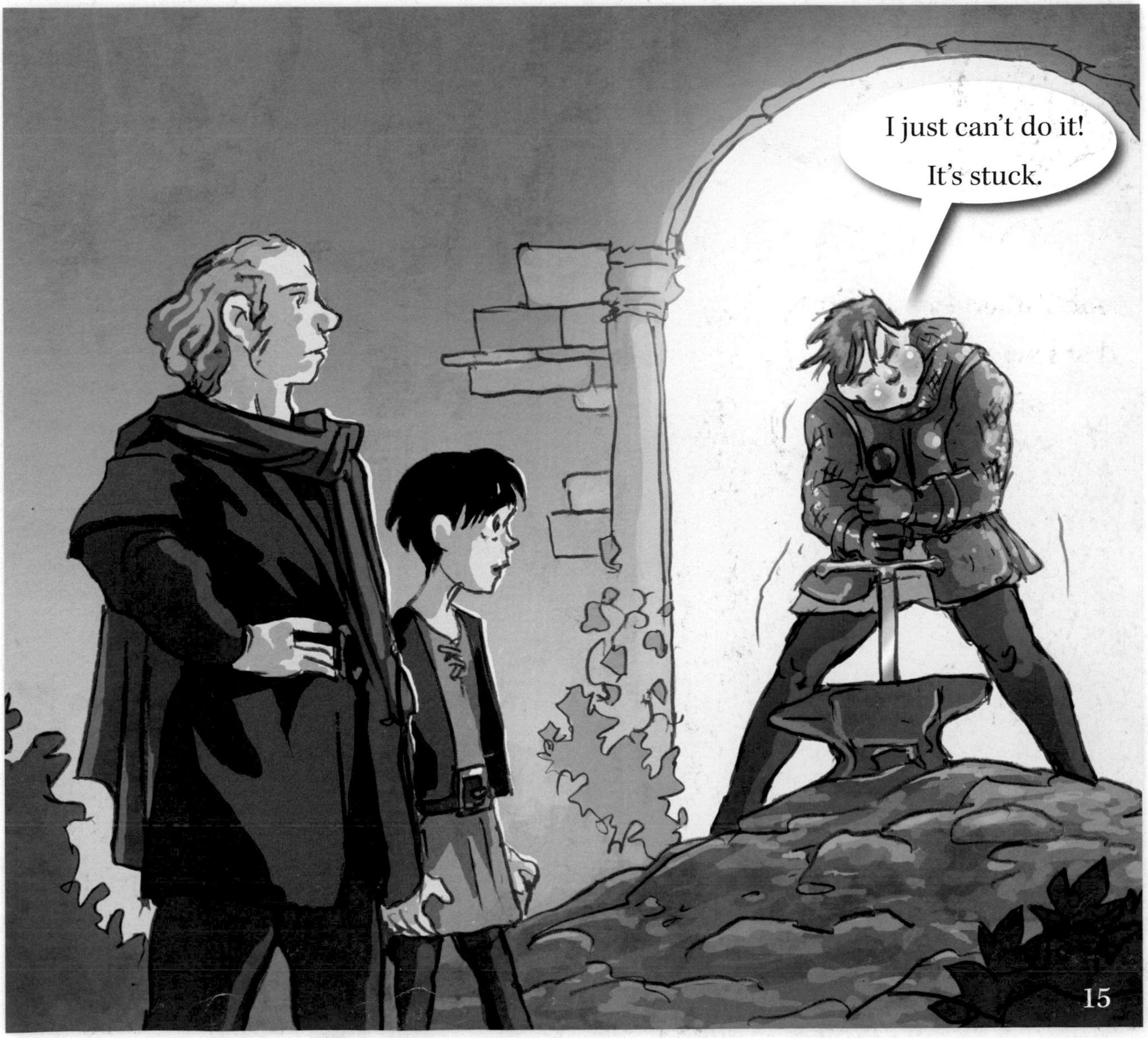
I just can't do it! It's stuck.

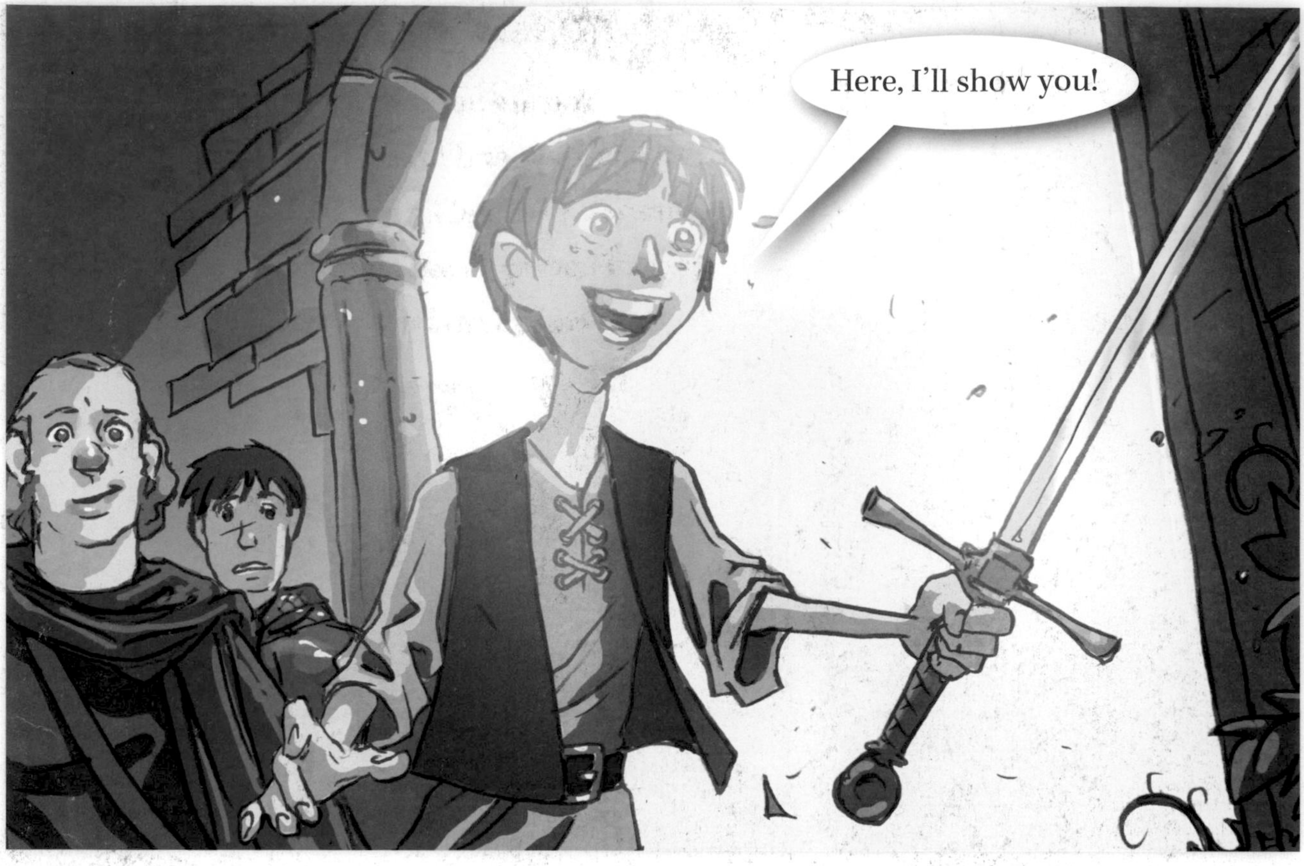
Here, I'll show you!

When Ector saw what Arthur could do, he knelt on the frosty ground and made Kay do the same.

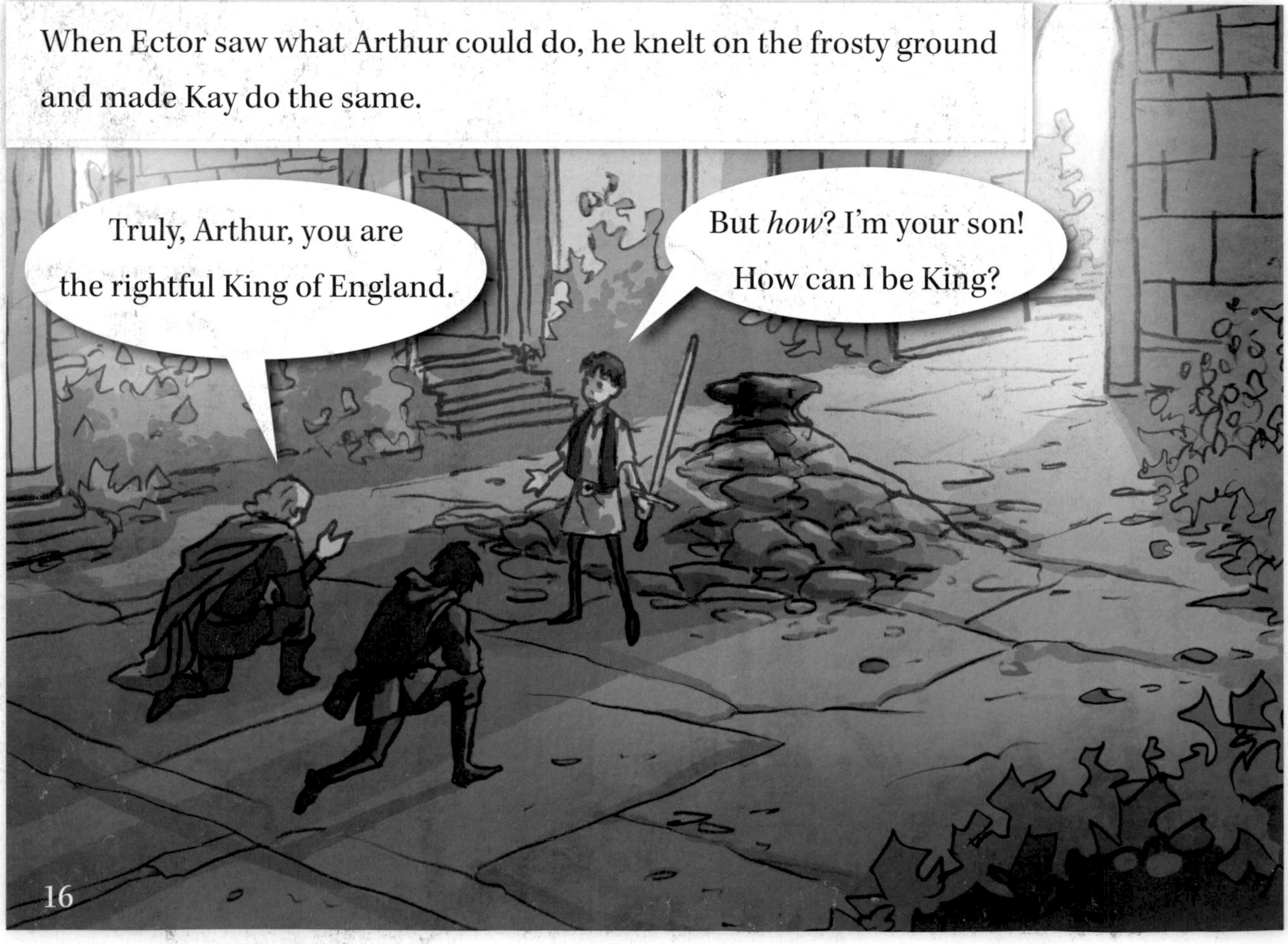
Truly, Arthur, you are the rightful King of England.
But *how*? I'm your son! How can I be King?

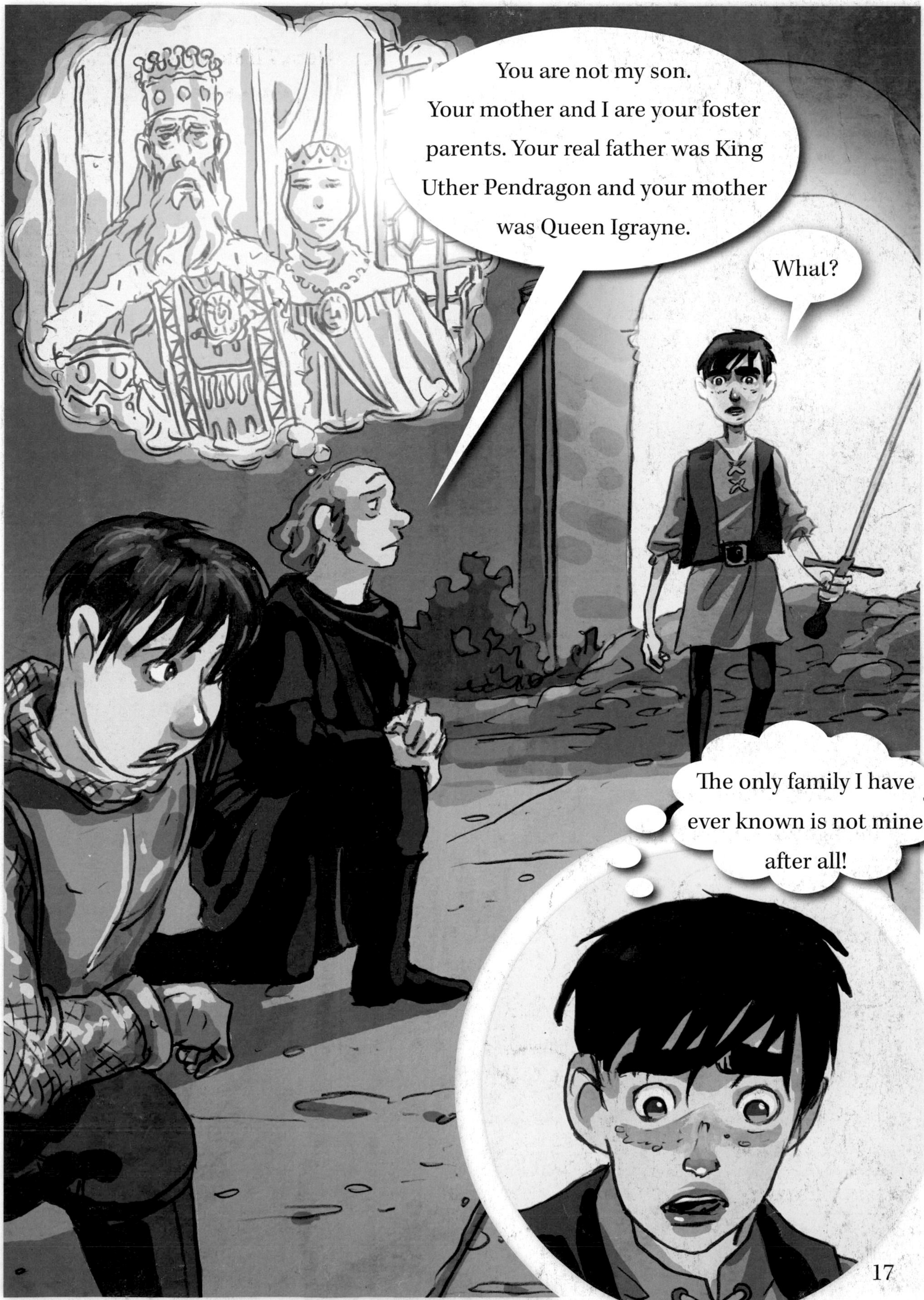
You are not my son. Your mother and I are your foster parents. Your real father was King Uther Pendragon and your mother was Queen Igrayne.
What?
The only family I have ever known is not mine after all!

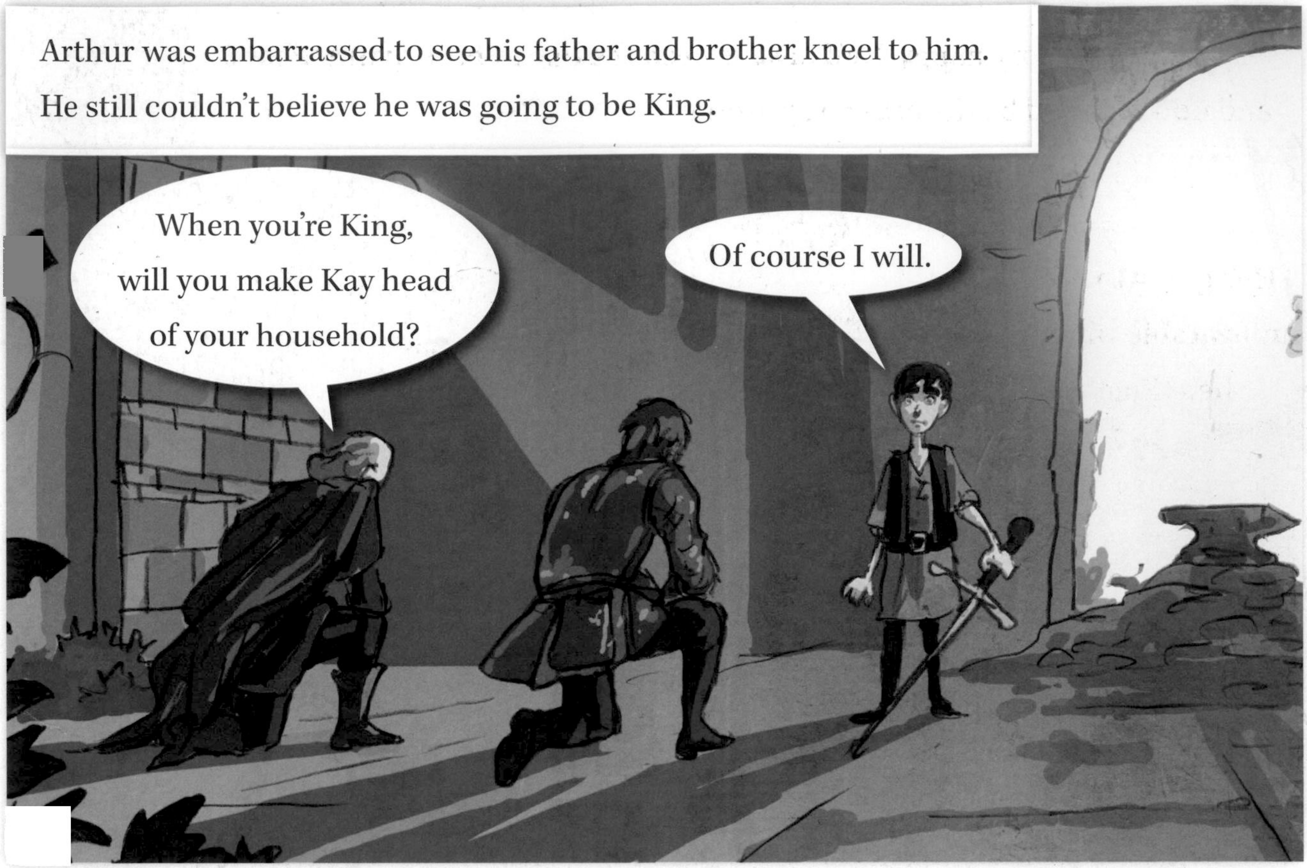
Arthur was embarrassed to see his father and brother kneel to him. He still couldn't believe he was going to be King.
When you're King, will you make Kay head of your household?
Of course I will.

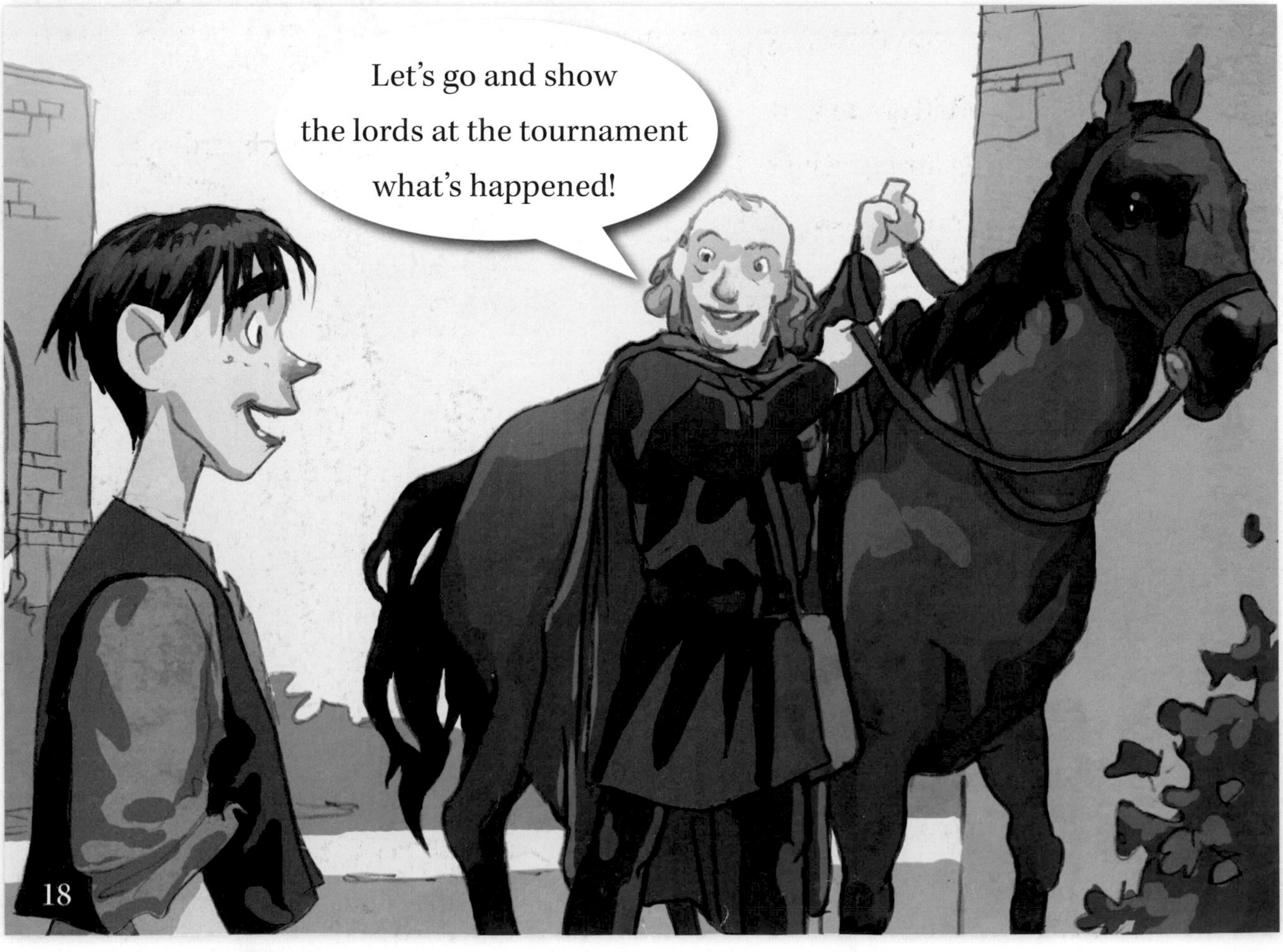
Let's go and show the lords at the tournament what's happened!

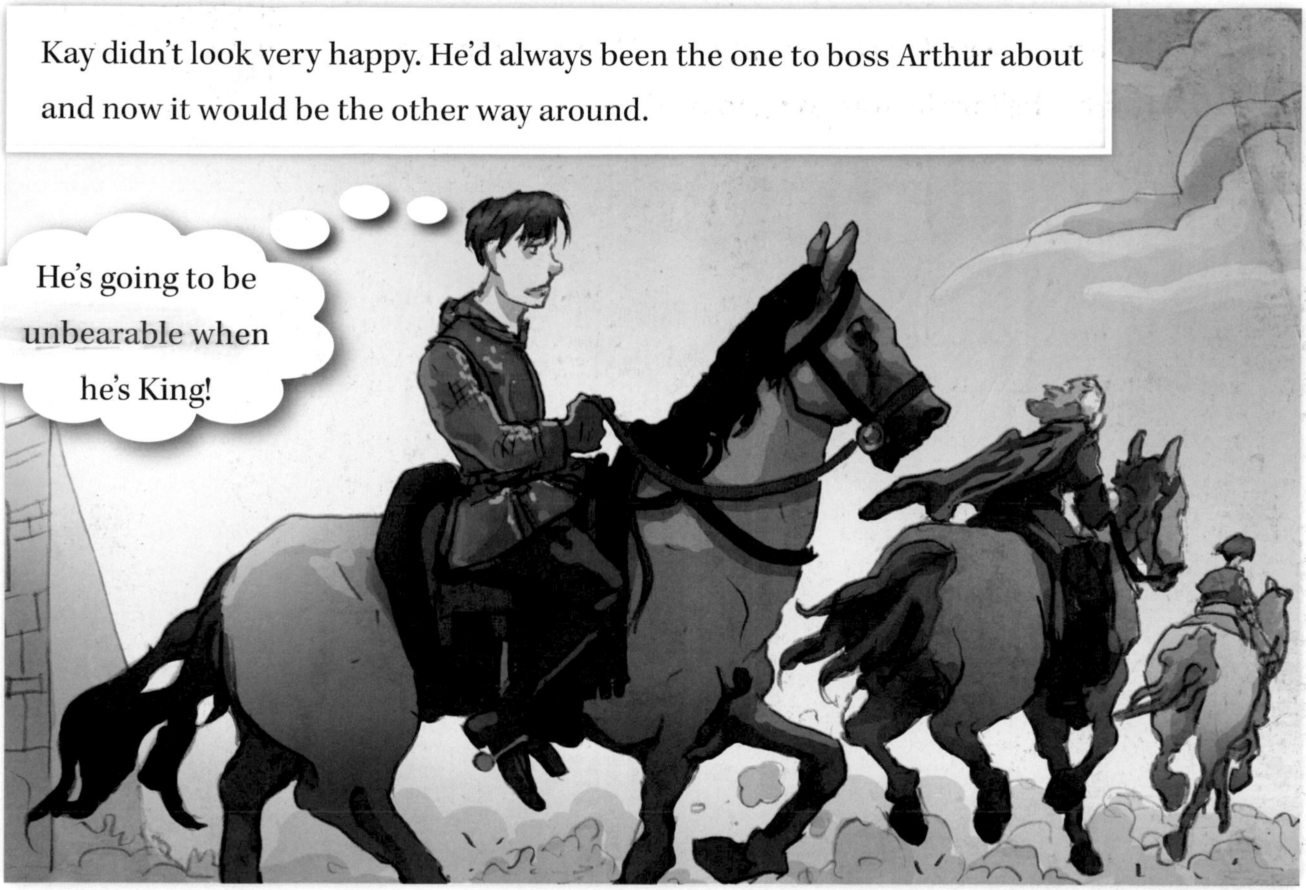
Kay didn't look very happy. He'd always been the one to boss Arthur about and now it would be the other way around.
He's going to be unbearable when he's King!

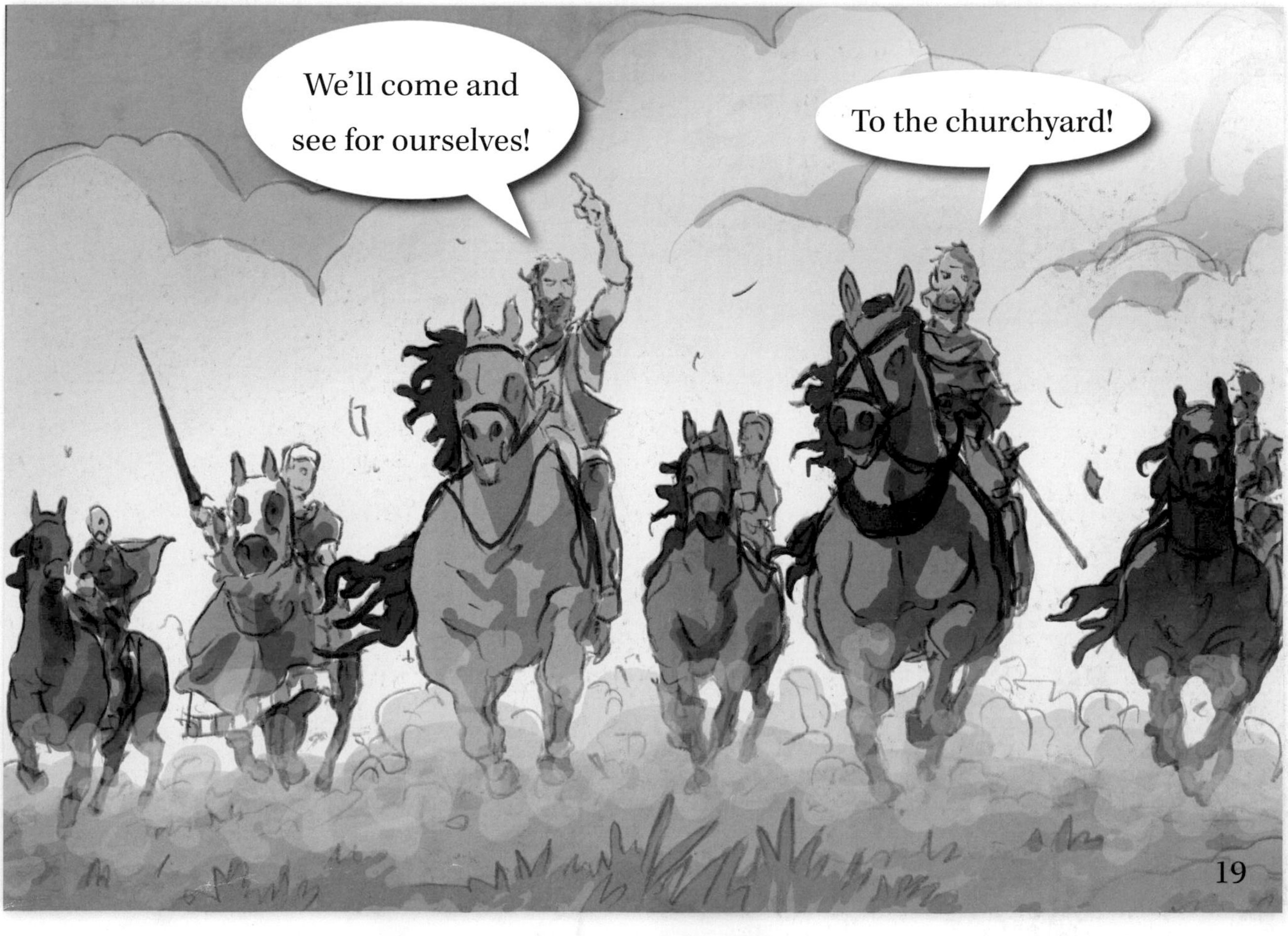
We'll come and see for ourselves!
To the churchyard!

The knights and lords watched Arthur perform the miracle over and over again.

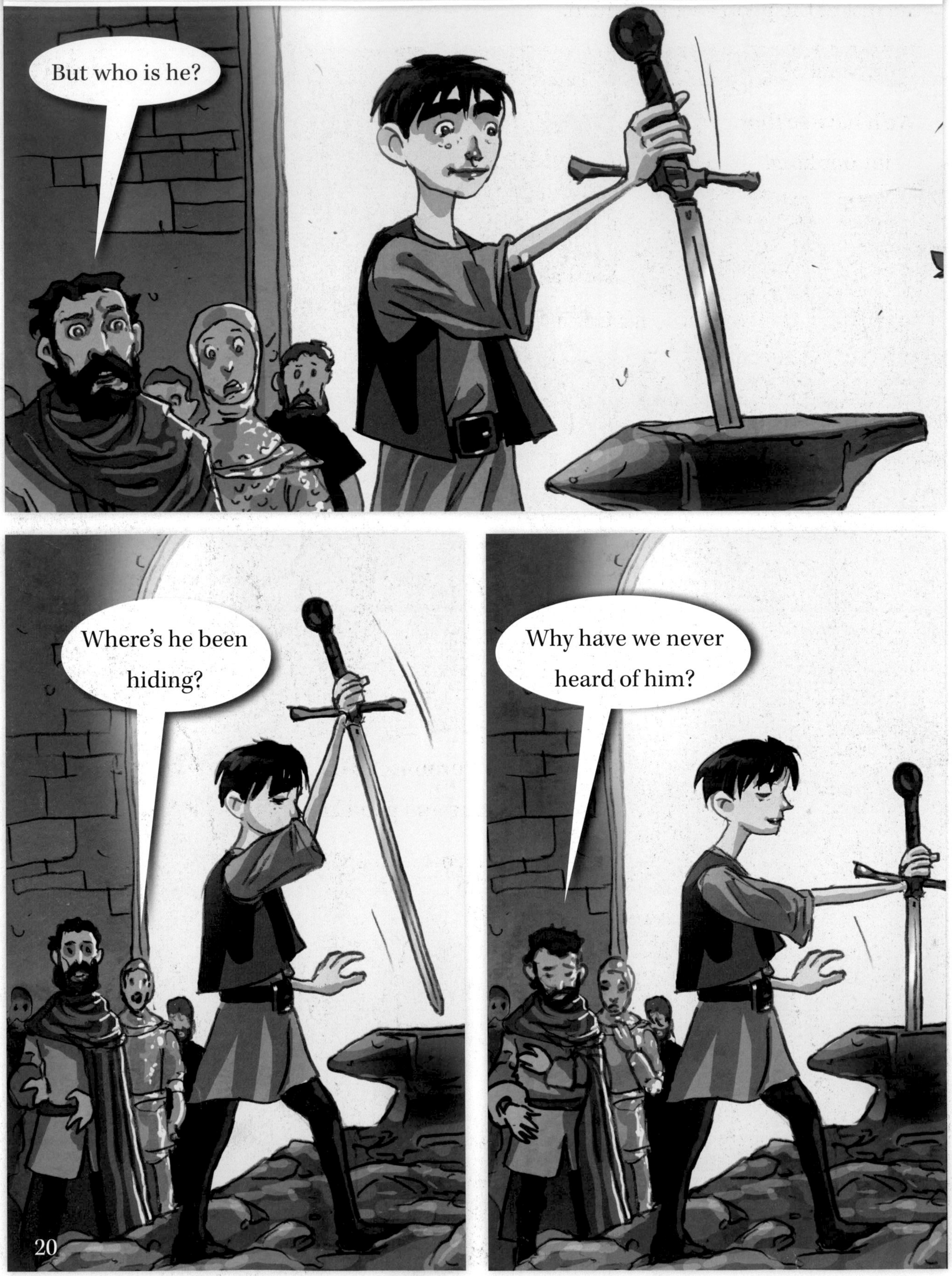
But who is he?
Where's he been hiding?
Why have we never heard of him?

The knights and lords didn't want to accept Arthur as king, but in the end it was the rest of the people who decided.

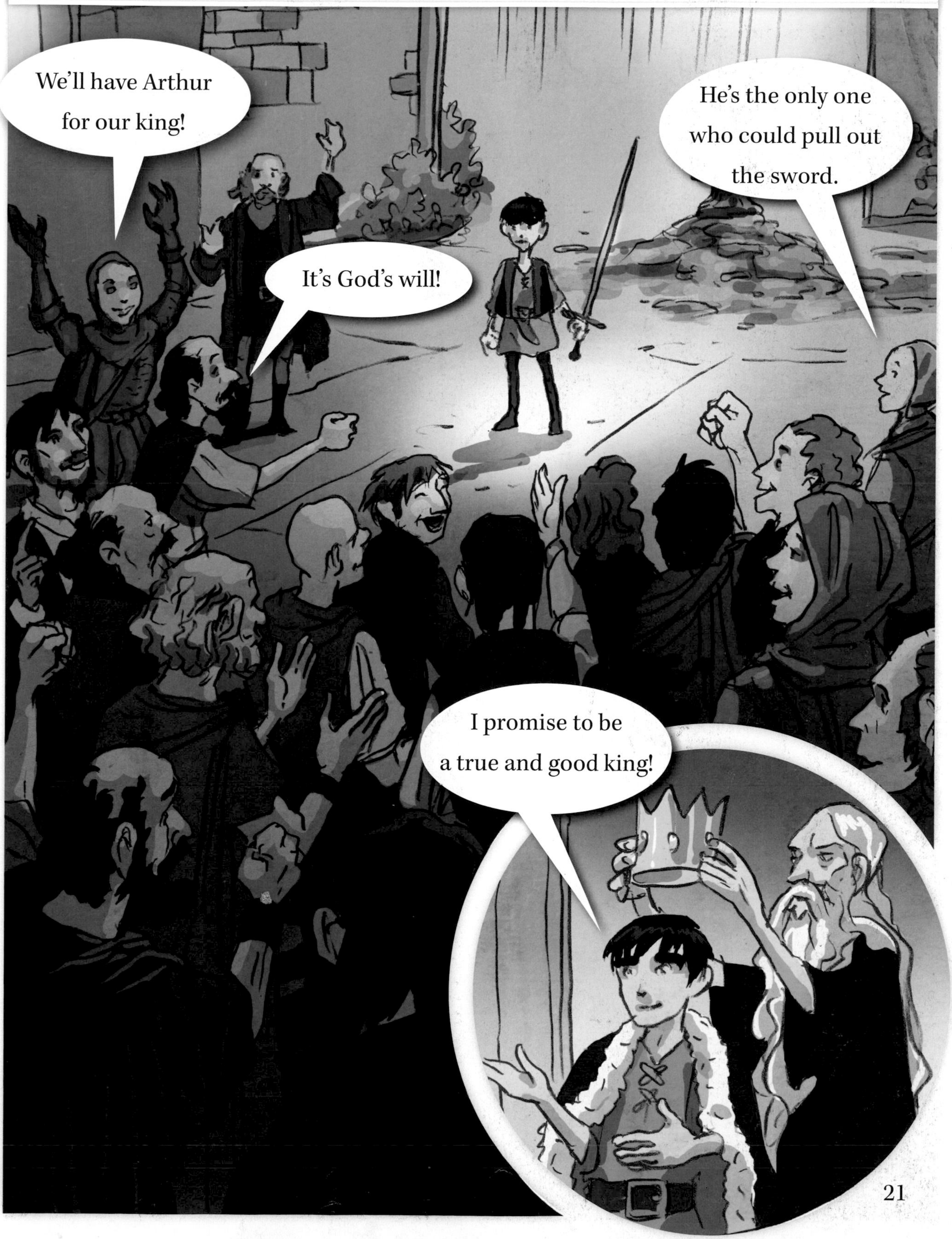
We'll have Arthur for our king!
It's God's will!
He's the only one who could pull out the sword.
I promise to be a true and good king!

The first thing Arthur did after he was crowned king was to keep his promise to Sir Ector.

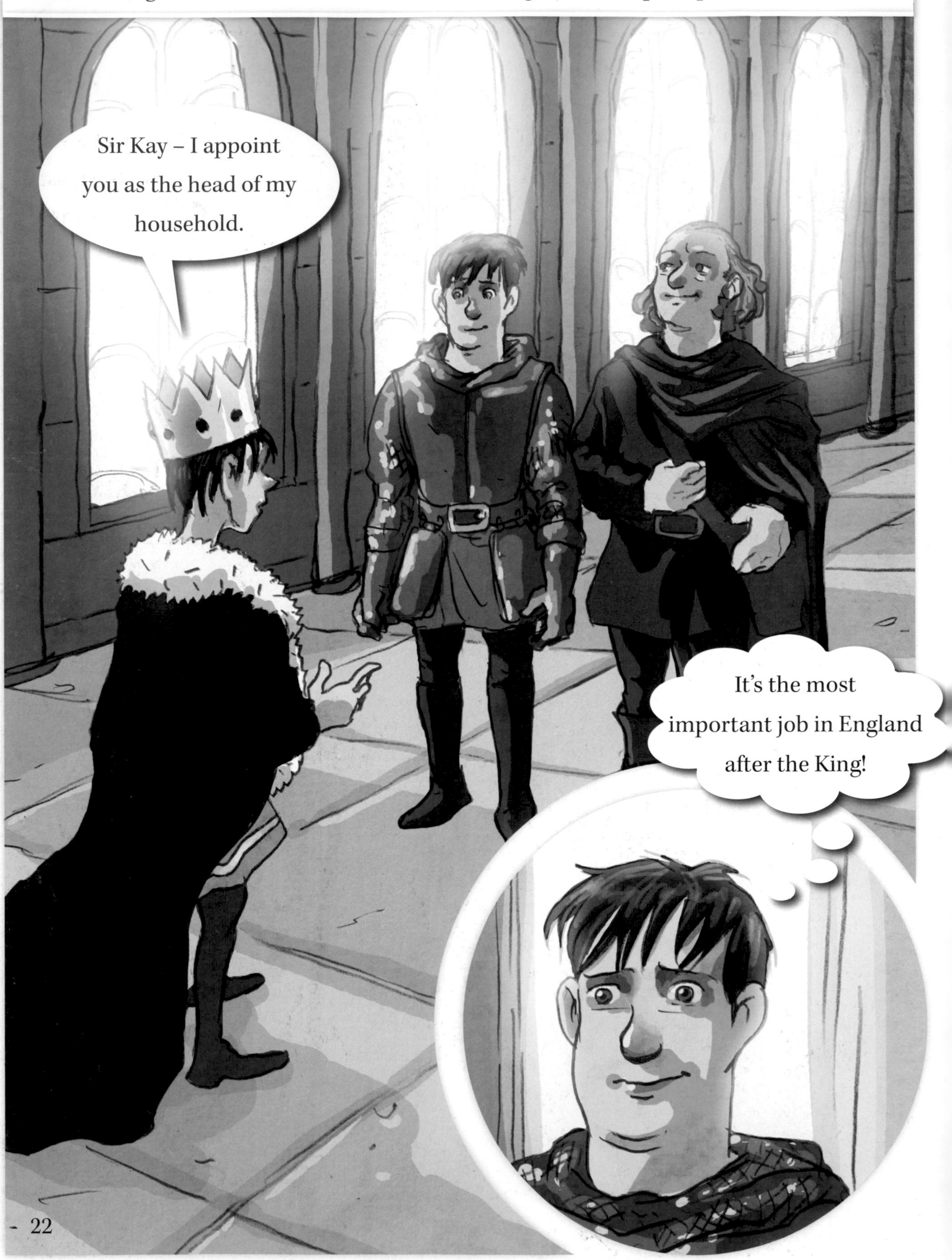
Sir Kay – I appoint you as the head of my household.
It's the most important job in England after the King!

Arthur was still only a boy, but a great feast was held in his honour. The kings of Scotland and other British regions came with hundreds of knights to join the celebrations.

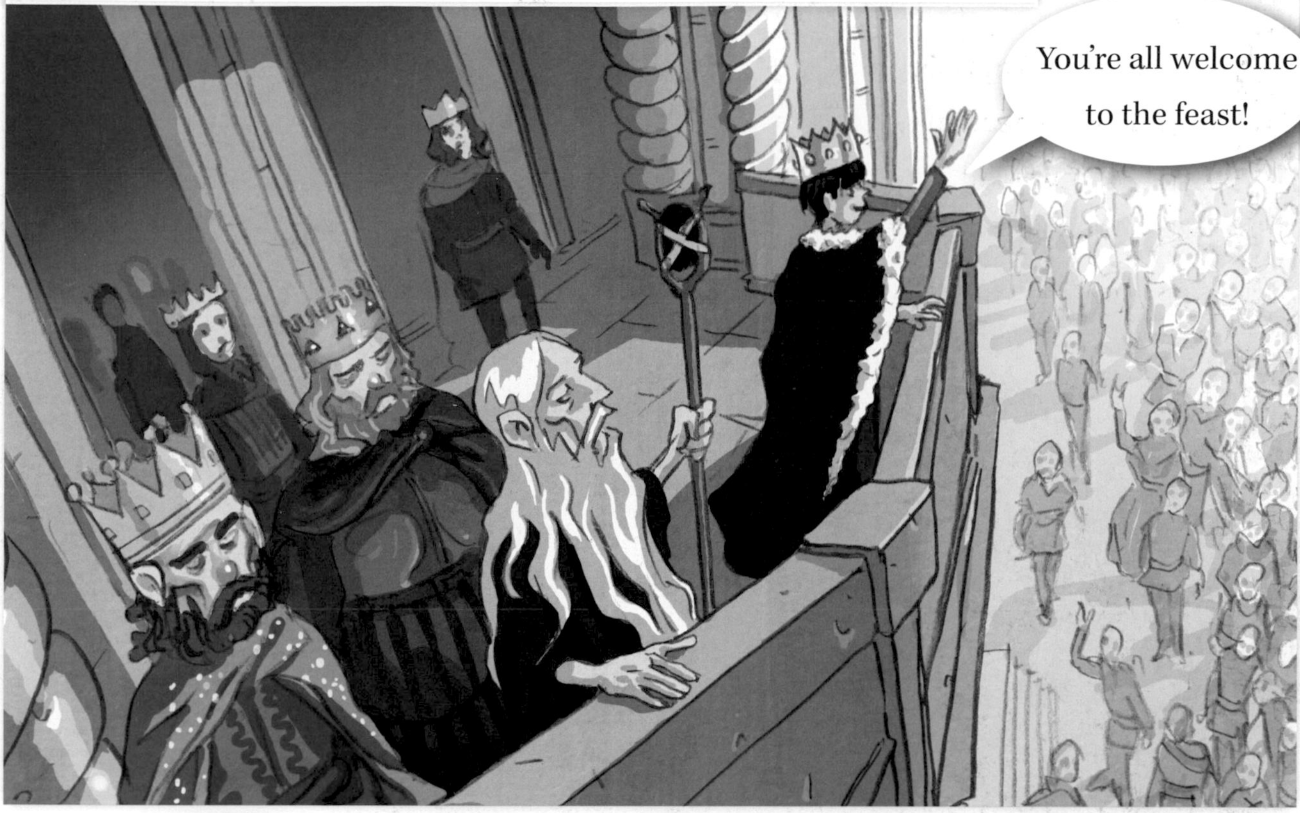
You're all welcome to the feast!

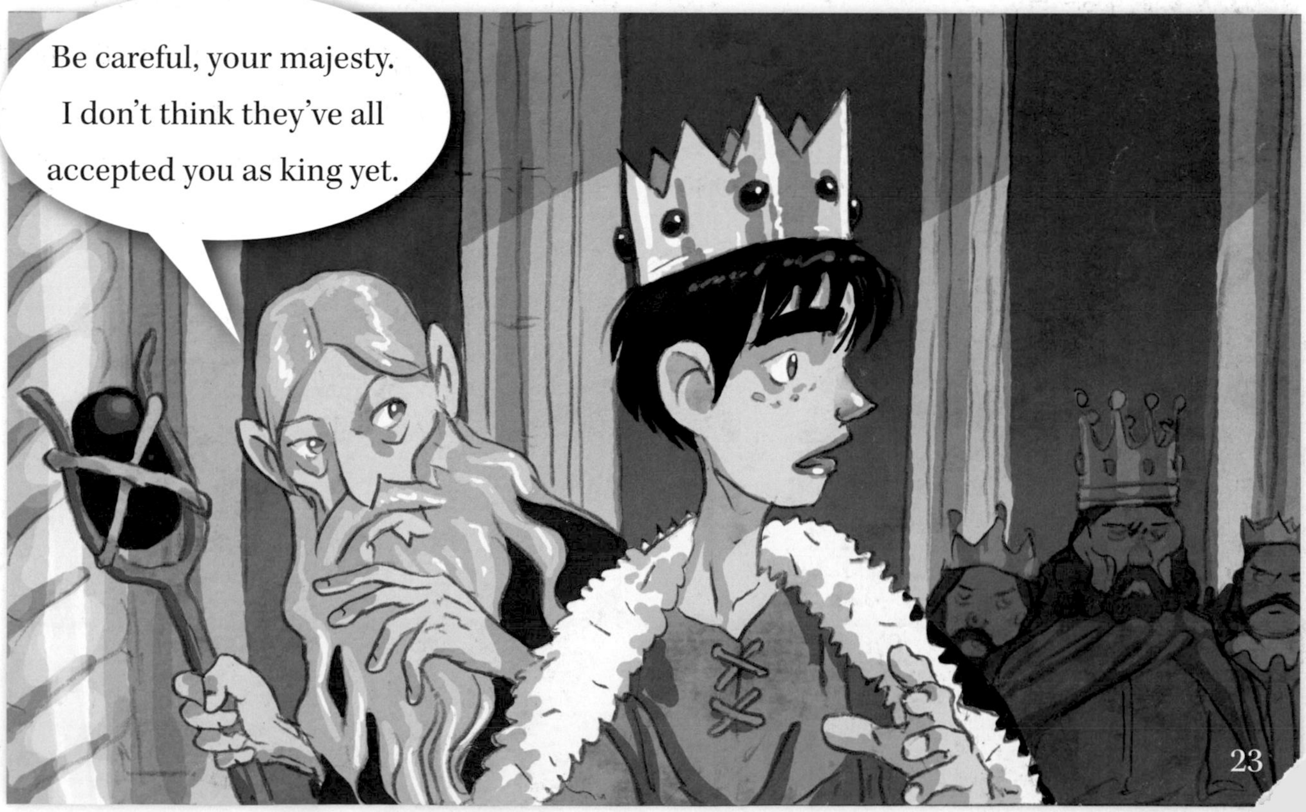
Be careful, your majesty. I don't think they've all accepted you as king yet.

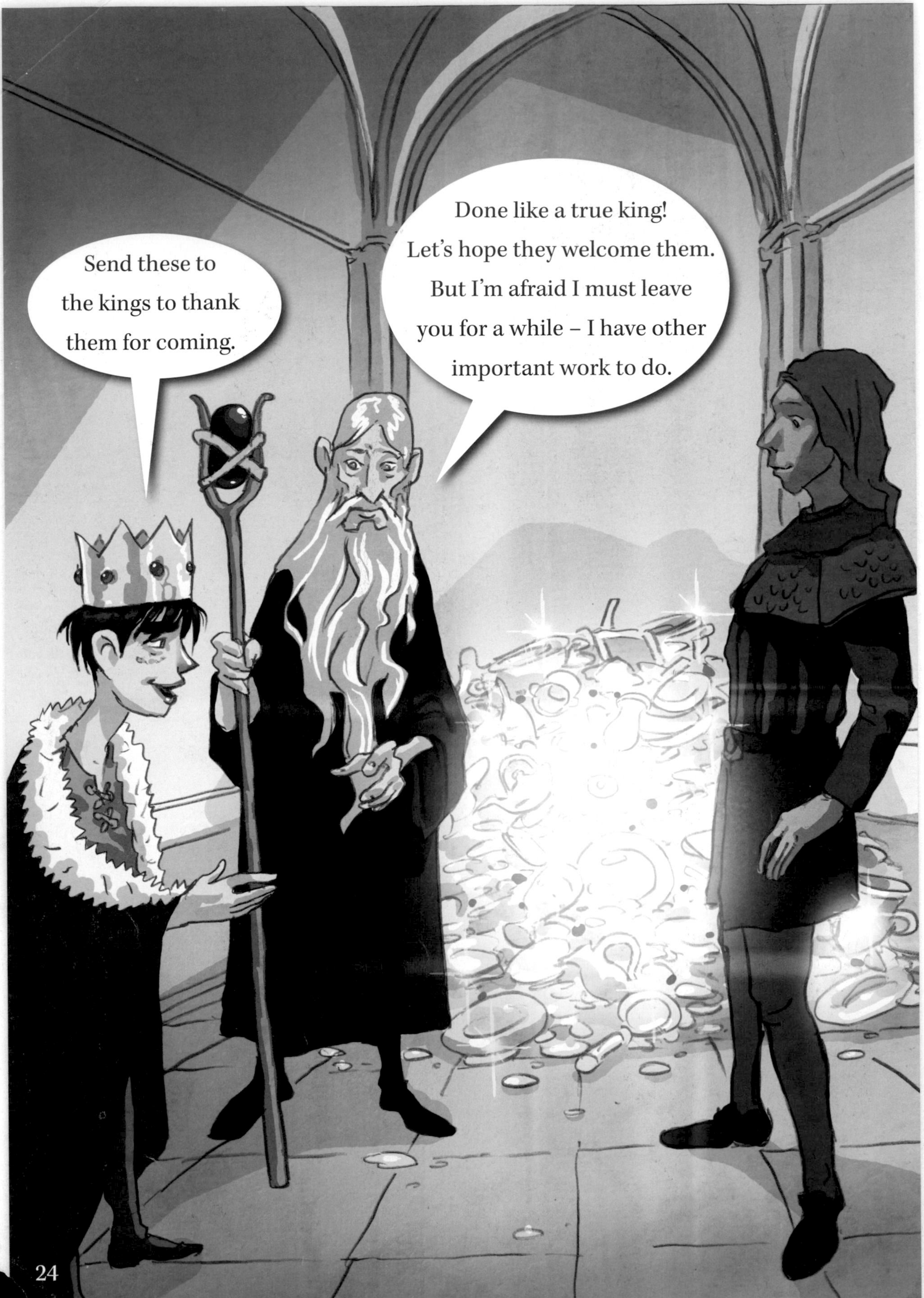
Send these to the kings to thank them for coming.
Done like a true king! Let's hope they welcome them. But I'm afraid I must leave you for a while – I have other important work to do.

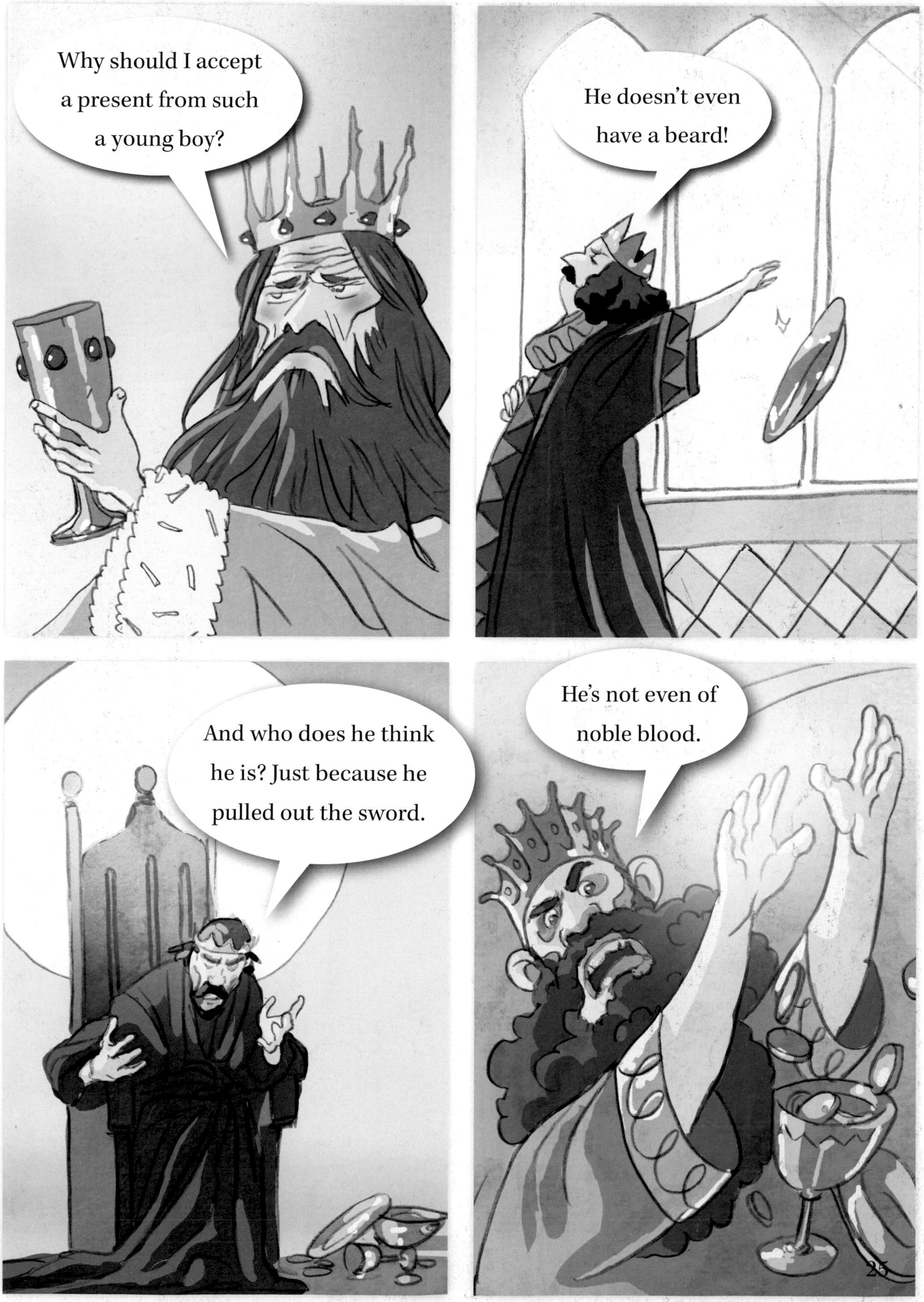
Why should I accept a present from such a young boy?
He doesn't even have a beard!
And who does he think he is? Just because he pulled out the sword.
He's not even of noble blood.

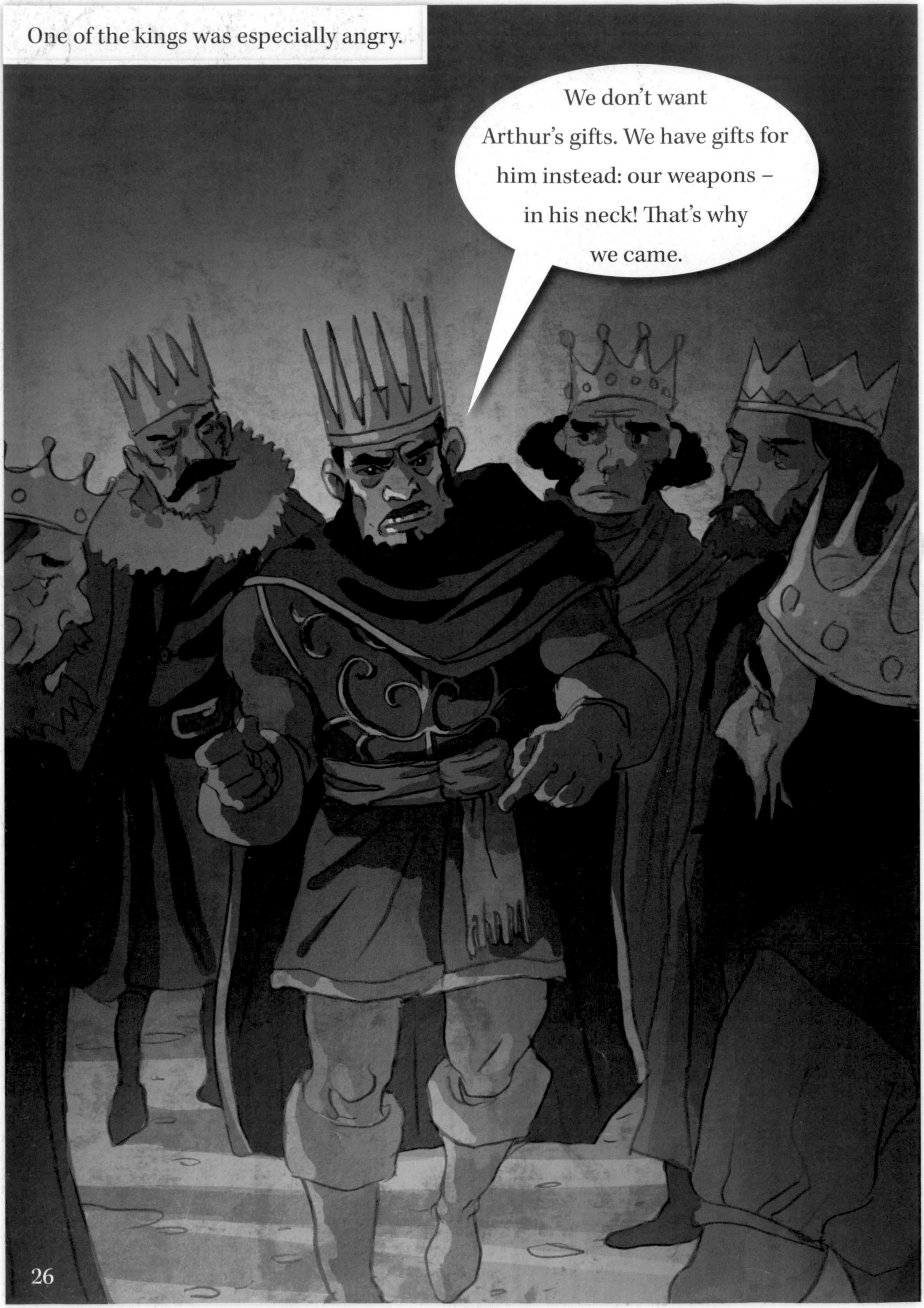
One of the kings was especially angry.
We don't want Arthur's gifts. We have gifts for him instead: our weapons – in his neck! That's why we came.

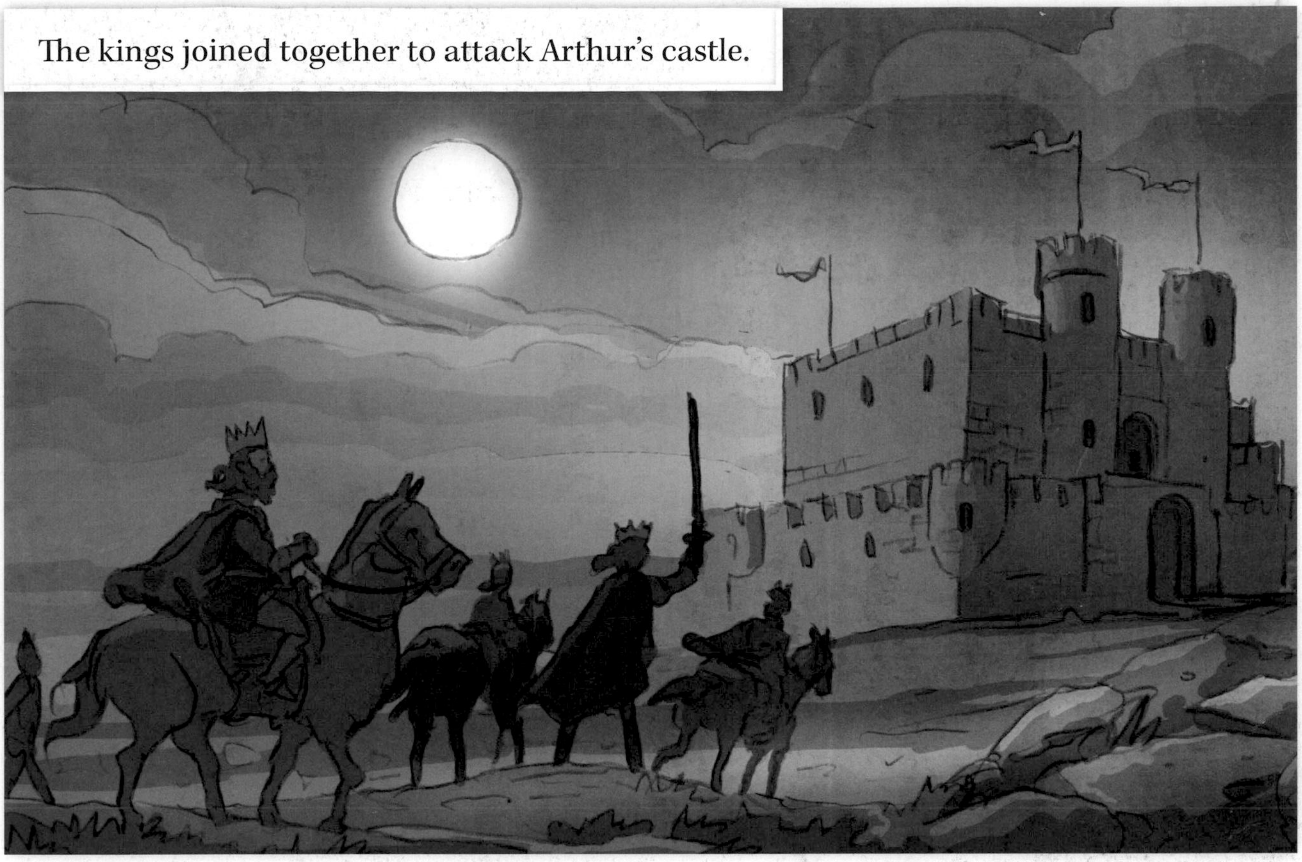
The kings joined together to attack Arthur's castle.

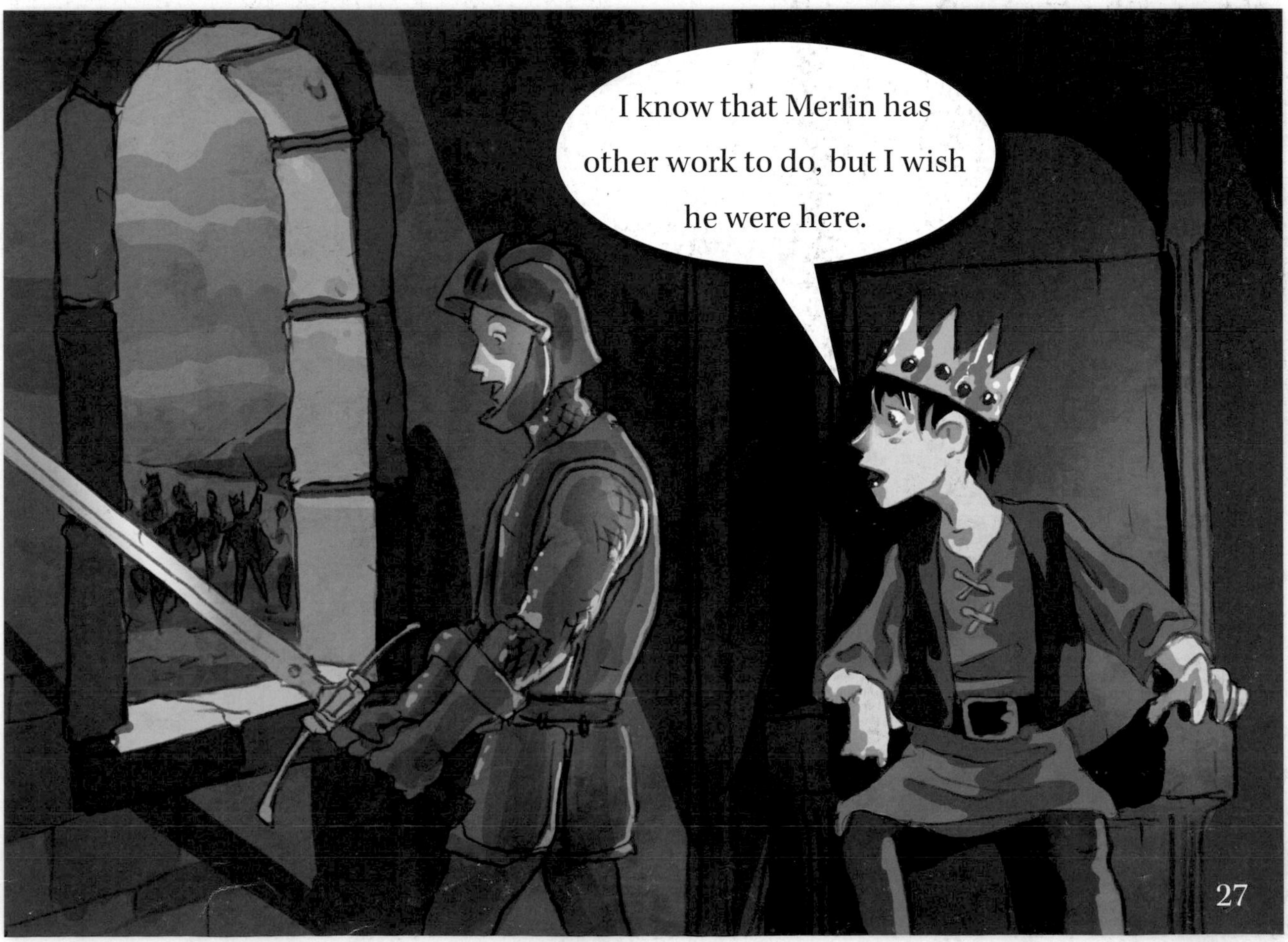
I know that Merlin has other work to do, but I wish he were here.

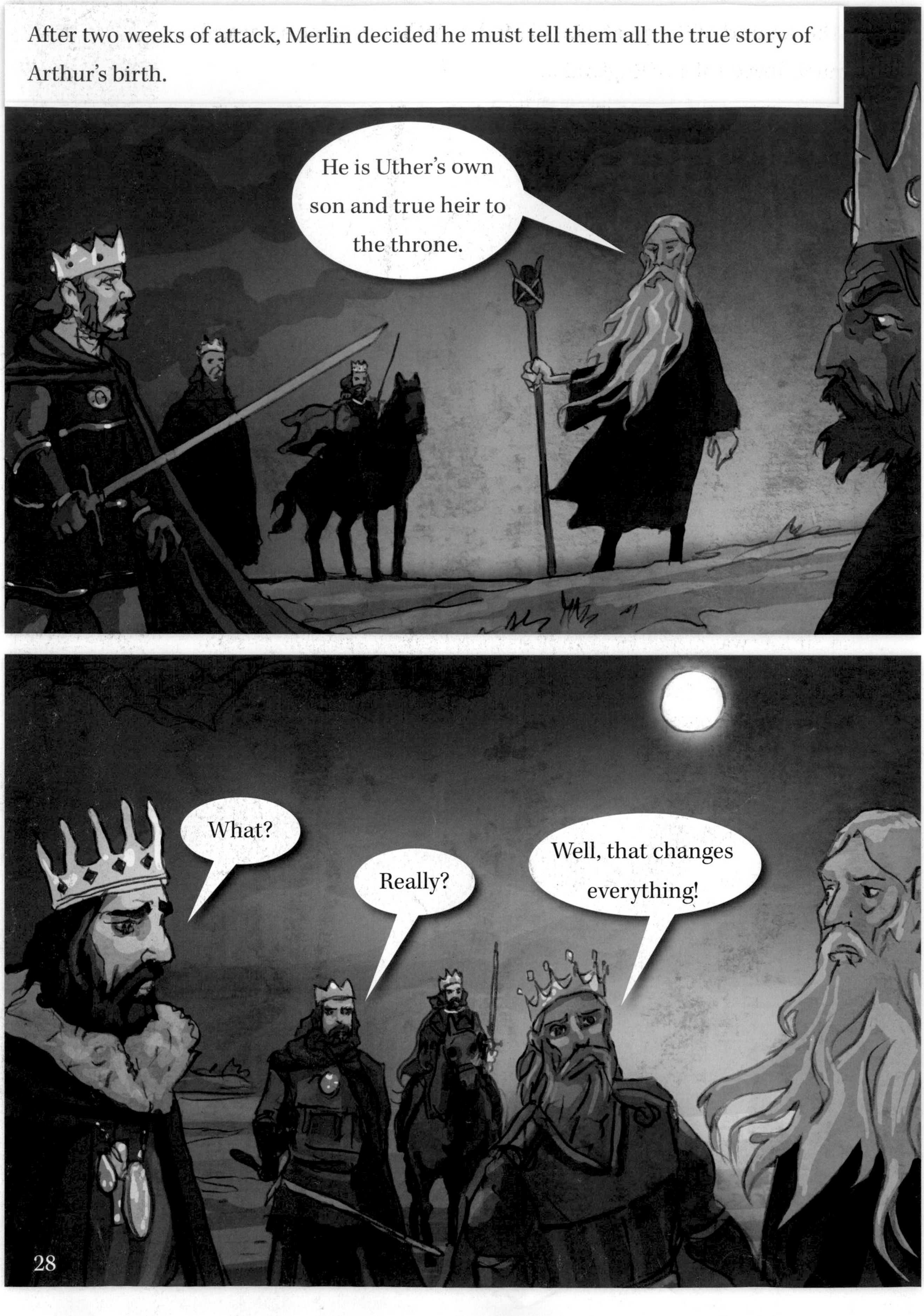
After two weeks of attack, Merlin decided he must tell them all the true story of Arthur's birth.
He is Uther's own son and true heir to the throne.
What?
Really?
Well, that changes everything!

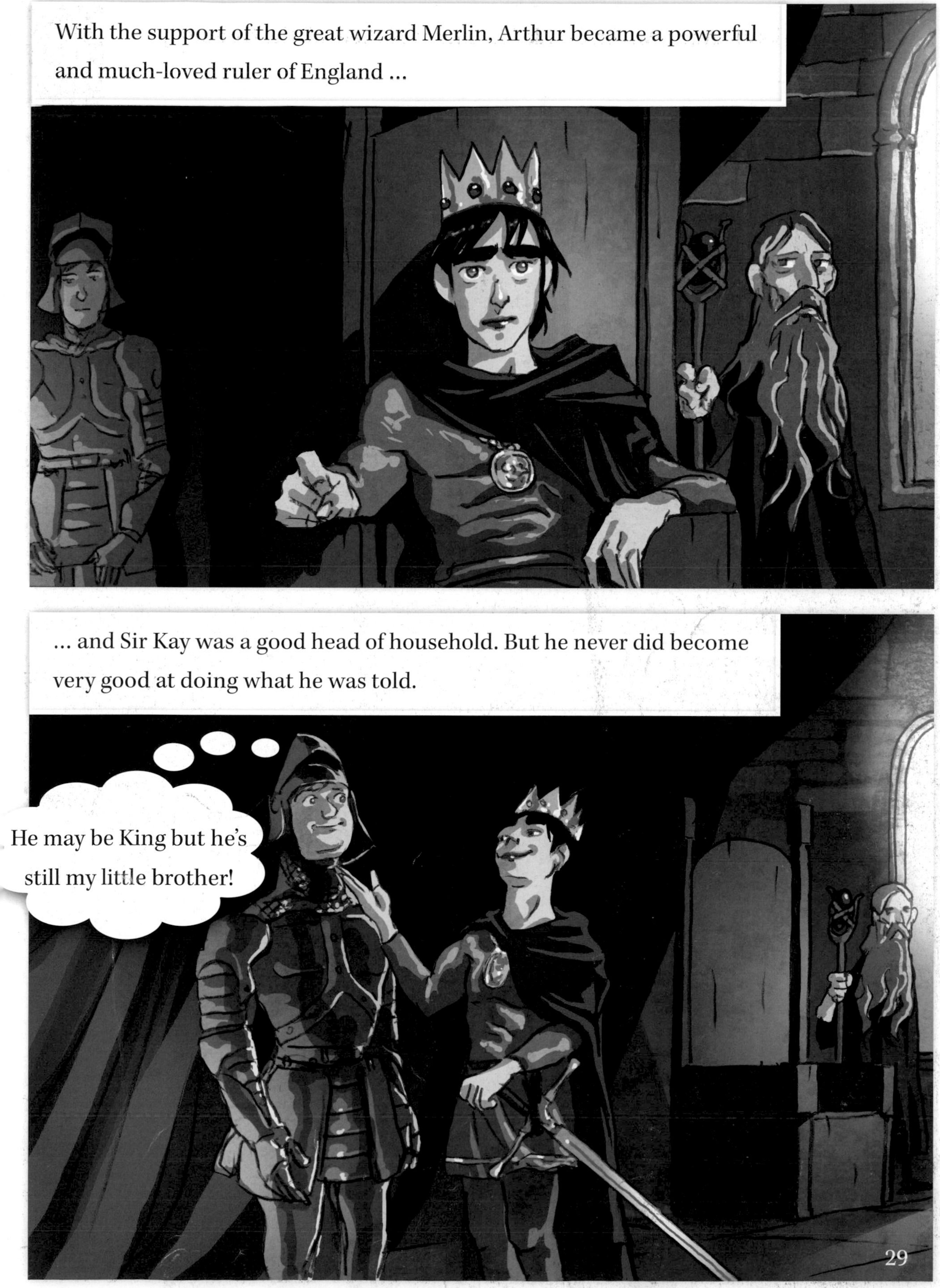
With the support of the great wizard Merlin, Arthur became a powerful and much-loved ruler of England ...
... and Sir Kay was a good head of household. But he never did become very good at doing what he was told.
He may be King but he's still my little brother!

A mysterious son

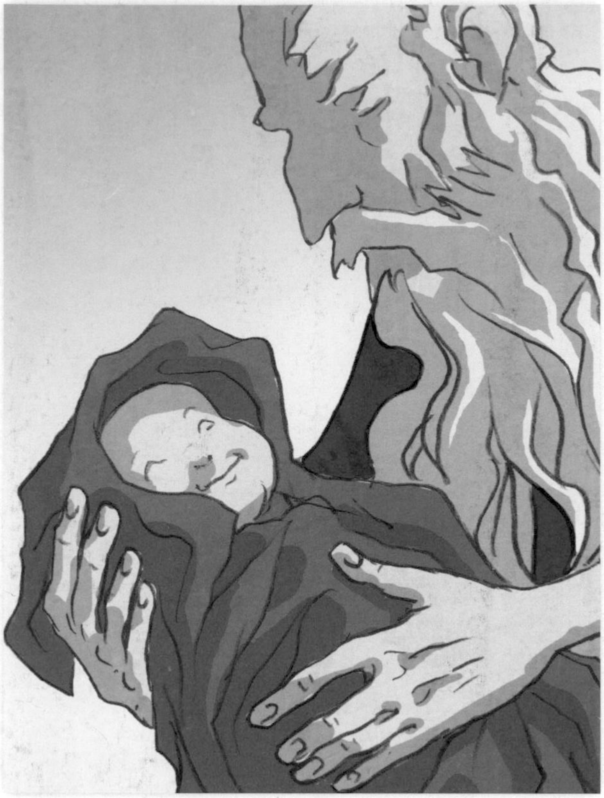

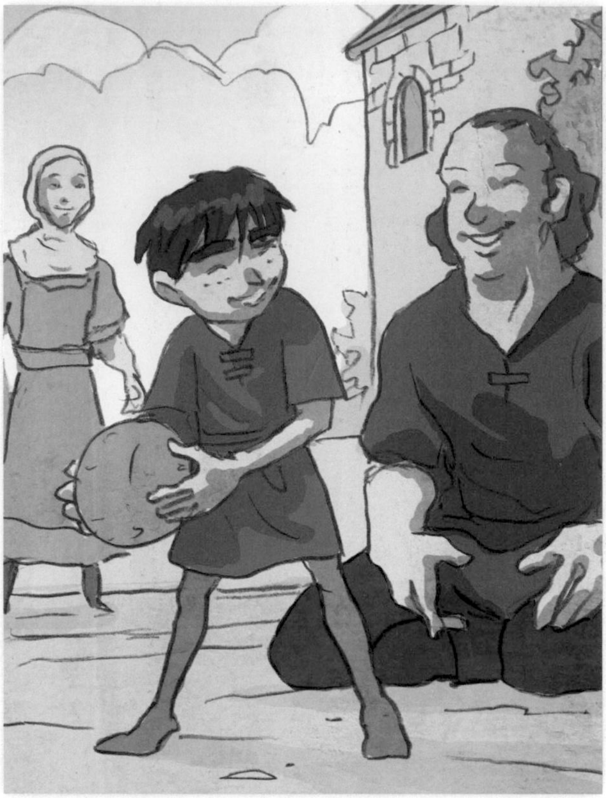

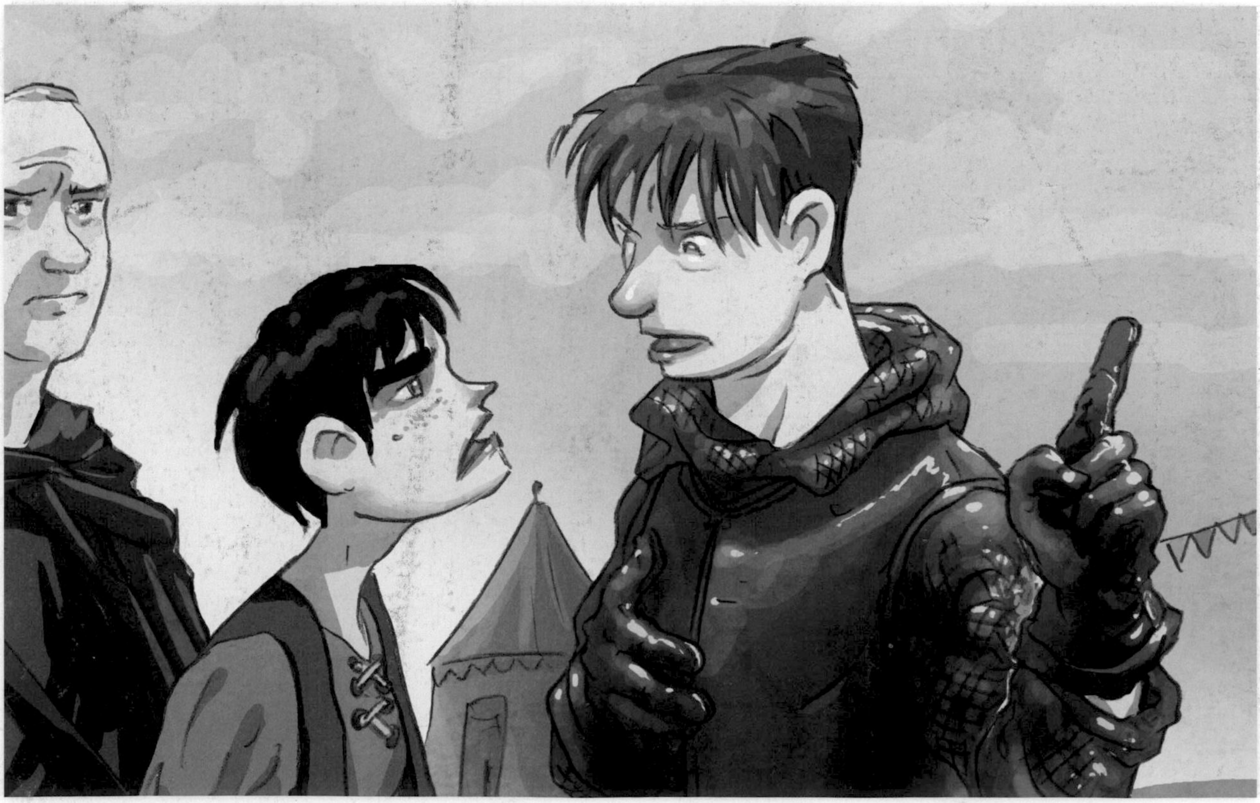

A famous king

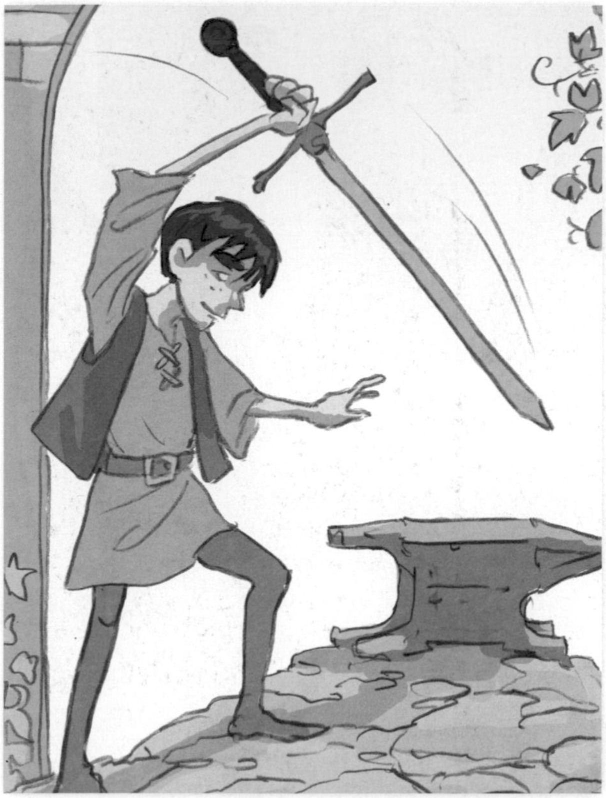

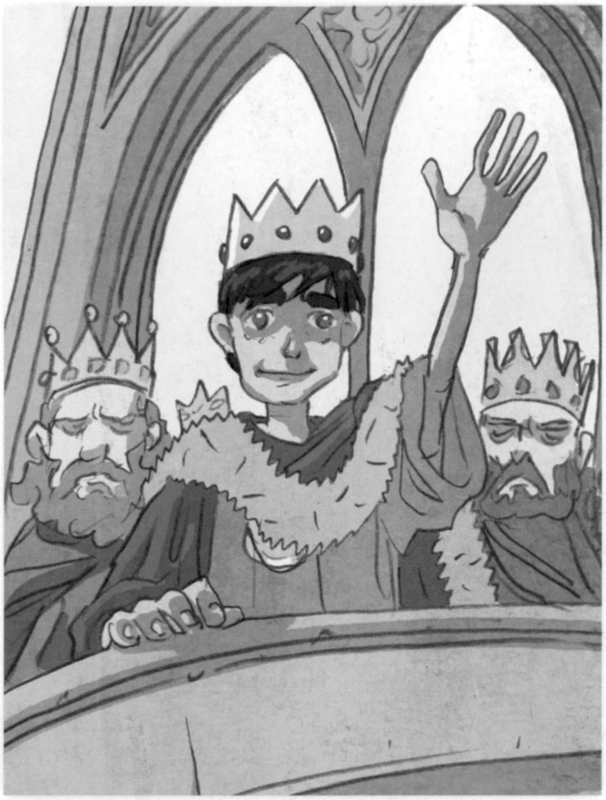

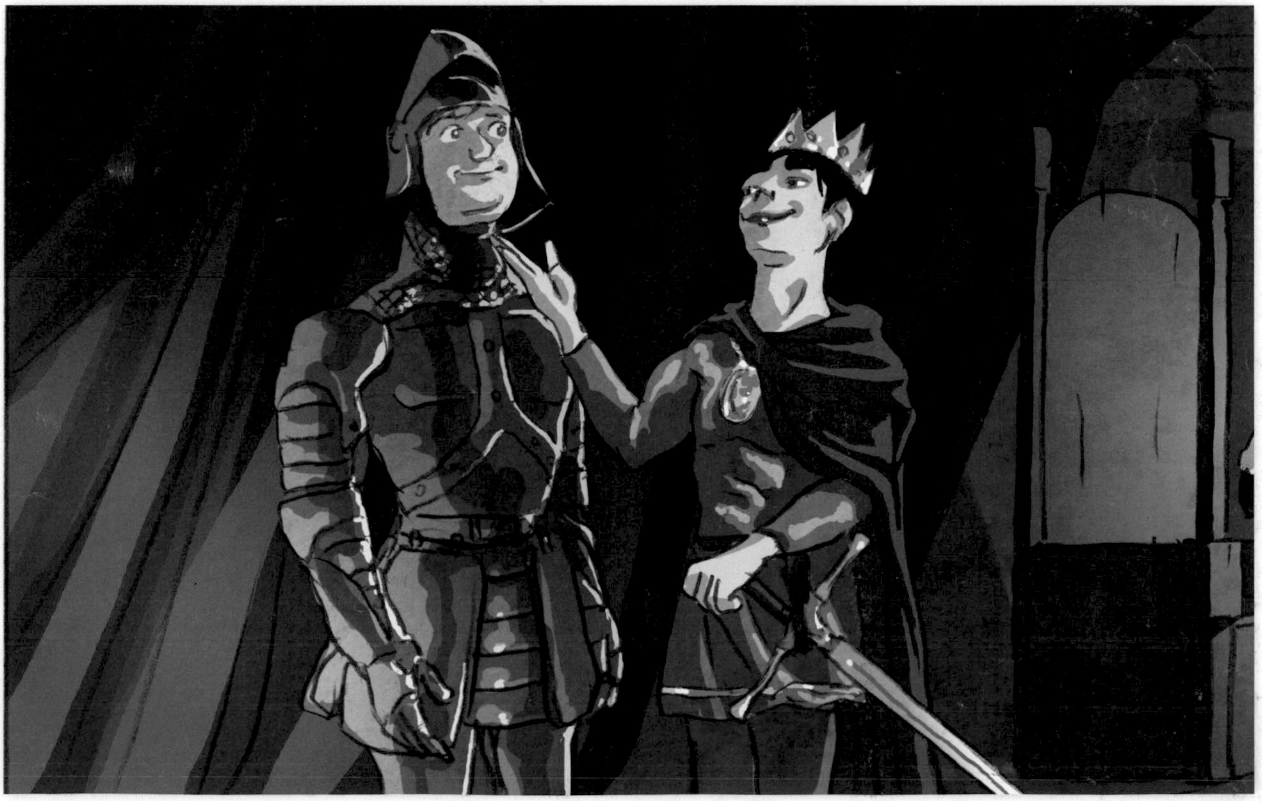

:paws: Ideas for reading :paws:

Written by Gillian Howell
Primary Literacy Consultant

Learning objectives: *(word reading objectives correspond with Lime band; all other objectives correspond with Sapphire band)* read most words quickly and accurately, without overt sounding and blending, when they have been frequently encountered; increasing their familiarity with a wide range of books, including myths, legends and traditional stories; drawing inferences such as inferring characters' feelings, thoughts and motives from their actions; predicting what might happen from details stated and implied

Curriculum links: History

Interest words: sword, knights, courage, miracles, centimetre, tournament, jousting, knelt, regions, celebrations, accept, weapons

Word count: 1,220

Resources: pens, paper, art materials, internet

Getting started

- Look at the cover and read the title together. Ask the children if they are familiar with the title and what they already know about this story. What is the boy doing? Turn to the back cover and read the blurb together to confirm the children's ideas.

- Look at the first page together. Explain that this is a graphic novel with a large and important part of the plot told through the illustrations and therefore they need to take careful notice of what is happening in the pictures and read the speech bubbles.

- Discuss with the children the names that are in the story and ensure they know how to pronounce them. Point out any new ones they may not know, e.g. *Uther Pendragon, Sir Ector.*

Reading and responding

- Ask the children to read the story together. Check that they understand the order in which to read the frames. On p2, point out the speech bubbles and encourage them to read these using an expressive tone.

- Point out *mounted* on p3 and check the children know what it means. Ask the children to suggest strategies they could use to work out words they find difficult, e.g. phonics, breaking longer words into chunks of words they already know and blending together, e.g. *Pendragon.*